Joseph Fownes

An enquiry into the principles of toleration

Second Edition

Joseph Fownes

An enquiry into the principles of toleration
Second Edition

ISBN/EAN: 9783337131807

Printed in Europe, USA, Canada, Australia, Japan

Cover: Foto ©Andreas Hilbeck / pixelio.de

More available books at **www.hansebooks.com**

A N

ENQUIRY

INTO THE

PRINCIPLES

OF

TOLERATION;

THE

DEGREE, in which they are admitted
by our LAWS;

AND THE

REASONABLENESS of the late APPLICATION
made by the DISSENTERS

TO PARLIAMENT

FOR AN

ENLARGEMENT of their RELIGIOUS LIBERTIES.

By JOSEPH FOWNES.

The SECOND EDITION, with confiderable ADDITIONS.

Quot adhuc repurgandæ latent leges, quas neque annorum nume-
rus, neque conditorum dignitas commendat, fed æquitas fola? et
ideo, cum iniquæ recognofcuntur, merito damnantur.

Tertulliani Apolog. cap. iv. p. 54. ed. Havercampi.

SHREWSBURY:
Printed by J. EDDOWES; and fold by J. BUCKLAND,
at No. 57, Pater-nofter-Row, LONDON. 1773.

Price Two Shillings and Six-pence.

PREFACE

To the FIRST EDITION.

THE plan of the following essay was laid, and the most material thoughts in it ranged under their respective heads, before the author had seen Mr. Mauduit's case of the dissenters. Upon looking into it, he found some of the topicks, which had been comprehended in his original design, insisted upon to great advantage; and for this reason has omitted several observations, which he intended to have made, that the reader might not be at the trouble of attending a second time, to what had been so much better said already. The writer hopes, therefore, that he shall not be considered by that ingenious gentleman in the light of a rival, but be received as an auxiliary: an auxiliary in support of a cause, which, as he has justly observed, is worthy of the efforts of all the friends of liberty to support it.

It

It was not till a great part, of what the author propofed to himfelf, was finifhed, that the letter to the diffenting minifters, who folicited parliament, fell into his hands. As two gentlemen of diftinguifhed learning and abilities' afe directly attacked; and in a manner called upon to defend themfelves, by the writer of that letter; and as it appeared highly probable, that one of them, at leaft, would undertake the viudication of himfelf, his brethren, and their caufe; it was at firft intended, to have taken no notice at all of that performance in this piece. But when that part of it, which relates more immediately to the diffenters, came to be confidered, the objections, which this gentleman has made to their conduct, lay fo continually and directly in the way, that it was found impoffible not to make fome animadverfions on his reprefentations and reafonings. This has made fome confiderable alteration in the form, which this head of the work would otherwife have worn, and added fomething to the length of it. Who the writer of the letter is, it would perhaps be thought difrefpectful to conjecture. He has affumed no character, which requires or warrants any particular kind of reference; and therefore he is all along mentioned only as a writer. A confiderable mafter of eafy and elegant compofition, he certainly is; and, as it

is

is hoped his meaning has not been miftaken,
(defignedly mifreprefented it affuredly has
not) fo, it is hoped, there is nothing in the
paffages, in which he is introduced, but
what is confiftent with the regard due to a
gentleman of abilities and learning, and agree-
able to that temper, which ought always
to be preferved in controverfial writings.
With whatever freedom any of his arguments
have been confidered, care has been taken to
do it with decency; and not to have confidered them with freedom would have been
injuftice to the caufe, which is here pleaded.

The whole of this performance was finifhed, and put into the printer's hands, before
a fight of Dr. Kippis's very fenfible defence
of the diffenters was obtained : fo that very
little, if any, alteration could be produced, in
what had been written, by the perufal of it.
One thought, towards the conclufion of this
tract, was inferted, while the fheets were work-
ing off, which was fuggefted by the Doctor's
book, of which an acknowledgement is made
at the bottom of the page in which it occurs.
The author gladly takes this opportunity of
returning his thanks to the Doctor for the
great pleafure received from his book.

It is only neceffary for the author to
add, with his predeceffors in publication,
Dr. Kippis and Mr. Mauduit, that what he
has here drawn up, was drawn up without
being

being communicated to a single diffenting
minifter. He entered upon the fubject un-
folicited and uninfluenced by any motive,
but the defire of doing juftice to a good
caufe. He hopes there will be nothing found
in his performance unfuitable to the temper
of one who is a friend to truth, and to religious liberty ;—who honours all, in whofe
attention the facred rights of confcience find
a place ;—who is a fteady friend to chriftianity, and an hearty well-wifher to the fuccefs of all attempts to promote it by example, argument and perfuafion ;—but an
enemy to all meafures of violence and perfecution. Thefe are the characters he will
always be defirous to maintain : and thefe
characters alone would dictate the fentiments
he has here committed to writing, though
he were utterly unconnected with any religious body in the kingdom. They are, indeed, no other fentiments than what Mr.
Locke, though no diffenter, nor attached to
any of their fentiments, (any farther than he
approved the general principles, upon which
they went, as the principles of that liberty
in which all chriftians ought to ftand faft,)
has delivered in his preface to his letter on
Toleration. The circumftances, which gave
occafion to fome of his expreffions, have, it
muft be gratefully owned, long fince ceafed
to exift among us : and thefe expreffions are

pre--

preferved here for this caufe only, that they
could not well be feparated from thofe, which
are adjoining to them ; and without the leaft
intention of making the moft diftant application of them to any perfons now living.
But, though his words had a fingular claim
to the regard of the times, in which he
lived, they are by no means unworthy of
the attention of the prefent, or indeed of
any times whatfoever, in which this queftion
is under confideration.

" Narrownefs of fpirit, on all fides, has
" undoubtedly been the principal occafion of
" our miferies and confufions. But, whatever
" may have been the occafion, it is now
" high time to feek for a thorough cure. —
" It is neither declarations of indulgence,
" nor acts of comprehenfion, [alone] fuch
" as have been yet practifed or projected
" among us, that can do the work. — The
" firft will but palliate, the fecond encreafe
" our evil. Abfolute liberty, juft and true,
" equal and impartial liberty is the thing
" we ftand in need of. — I cannot therefore
" but hope, that this difcourfe, — demonftra-
" ting both the equitablenefs and practica-
" blenefs of the thing, will be efteemed
" highly feafonable by all men, that have
" fouls large enough to prefer the intereft
" of the publick before that of a party."
A glorious, and never to be forgotten ftep
was,

was, about that time, taken towards introducing this important blessing. Whether it
quite answered the idea of religious liberty,
which is pointed out in the above cited
words, let those, who have maturely confidered it, judge. And if it does not, I leave
them to judge also, whether, if this great
man were now living, and were to be asked
his opinion of the fitness of granting the
request of the dissenters, he would not give
it for going this step farther?

PREFACE

PREFACE

To the Second Edition.

AN account having been already given, in the preface to the firſt edition of this pamphlet, of the riſe and progreſs of it, nothing farther is neceſſary to be added here concerning it. The differences between the concluſion of this and the foregoing edition will be eaſily accounted for by any one, who conſiders that at the time of this ſecond publication, the petition of the diſſenters was again laid before the parliament. This additional preface, and the appendix, will ſufficiently explain themſelves; and all, which remains farther to be ſaid, concerning them, and the eſſay, to which they relate, is to recommend the reaſonings contained in them to the candid attention of ſuch as may peruſe them.

What apology may be needful for the whole, or any part, of the enſuing enquiry, the readers of it will determine by their own judgment. That, which the author himſelf apprehended, at the writing of it, might be

a   thought

thought moſt liable to exception, was his employing ſo many pages in attempting to eſtabliſh the general principles of Toleration, which had been ſo largely diſcuſſed by writers of the moſt diſtinguiſhed reputation. But according to his views of the affair, which gave occaſion for his book, ſuch a conſideration of them ſeemed unavoidable. The more he reflected on the diſappointment of the diſſenters, the more he was convinced, that it could be reaſonably founded only on one of the following ſuppoſitions : — that Toleration is not a matter of right, but of favour ; — that, allowing it to be a matter of right, the penal laws againſt diſſenters are no infringement of that right ; *i. e.* are not perſecuting laws ; — that if they are perſecuting laws, the act of Toleration is an exemption from them, adequate to the relief of all, who need to be exempted from them ; — or, laſtly, that there was ſomething in the nature of the requeſt made by the diſſenters, which rendered the farther exemption, which they ſolicited from theſe laws, unreaſonable. That the act of Toleration affords but a very imperfect protection from the ſeverity of theſe ſtatutes, is a plain matter of fact, which admits of no diſpute. But how far the laws, of which it is a mitigation, are in themſelves unjuſtifiable ; or whether there was any thing peculiar in that

ſecurity

fecurity from them, for which the diffenters became fuitors, which rendered their cafe unworthy of regard, muft be determined by an appeal to the original principles of Toleration. For this reafon it was thought indifpenfably requifite to ftate them, and collect all the fubfequent parts of this queftion into one point of view with this leading, capital part of all; that, by the light which it muft of neceffity caft upon the others, the equity of the relief requefted by the diffenters might be clearly determined. And, if it has appeared, upon a careful furvey, that Toleration is the right of all good fubjects, and members of fociety;—if it is found, that the penal laws againft diffenters are utterly fubverfive of this right, and, confequently, unjuft;—and, if it has been made evident, that the principles and deportment of the diffenters, and the affurances, which they are ready to give to the ftate for their loyal and unexceptionable demeanor, are fuch as ought, in reafon, to obviate all fufpicion of the contrary: if thefe things have been fatisfactorily fhewn, the inference makes itfelf, and is too plain and certain, not to be feen and acknowledged by every intelligent perfon;—that the requeft of the diffenters was reafonable, and that the part they acted in prefenting it was worthy to be approved.

a 2   When

When applications, for relief from burthens, are founded upon principles of juftice,
it is generally allowed that apprehenfions of
fome accidental, or merely poffible inconveniencies, with which granting the defired relief might be attended, are not of ftrength
fufficient to juftify the refufal of it. And
yet to this clafs the objections, which have
been urged againft the arguments by which
the diffenters have defended their caufe, muft,
in general, be reduced. — Alarming hints
have been given of the dangers, which might
have followed, if their defire had been
granted. — Great refpect has been expreffed
for the prefent diffenters; but great doubt
concerning their conduct, and an unwilling-
nefs to anfwer for their behaviour, were they
to carry their point, have been joined with
thefe profeffions of refpect. — Vague and
obfcure prefages of evils, which, in this cafe,
might fome time arife, have been entertained
and fuffered to work upon the imagination;
and fuppofitions of events have been made, fo
chimerical and deftitute of foundation, that it
is furprizing that gentlemen of underftanding, fhould ever be impreffed by them. But
the groundleffnefs of thefe fuppofitions will
be confidered hereafter. What is now to be
obferved is, that all thefe reafonings proceed
upon an entire inattention to the nature of the
cafe, which they are defigned to affect. In
                                        matters

matters of mere favour, or expedience, such considerations as these may be allowed to have their weight; though, even in things of this kind, it is owned, that present and probable advantages ought to turn the scale against distant, and merely possible, disadvantages. But, in matters of right, such objections as these are seldom admitted. Were they suffered indeed to prevail, there is no liberty so important and reasonable, but it might be denied; no right so sacred and inviolable, but it might be taken away. For what right, what liberty is there which may not be abused? Or what advantage is there, from which some possible inconvenience may not result? The dissenters apprehend the relief, which they asked, was no more than the principles of reason, christianity, and protestantism, warranted them to request; yet such objections as those, which have been mentioned, seem to be with many considerable enough to overbalance all, which the petitioners could produce in support of their request; and to justify the retaining of laws, which even they who contend for their continuance, have not undertaken to vindicate; except it be by alledging, that they are laws not to be executed, but to stand in TERROREM only; an excuse, which is at once utterly insufficient to defend the keeping up of such laws; and, (as the argument has been conducted

ducted by thofe who have thought proper
to have recourfe to it) is, in effect, giving
up the caufe.

To be made in TERROREM, is the common character of all penal laws whatfoever.
The FIRST intention of them is to PREVENT
the forbidden actions, by the fear of the
penalties enacted on account of the violation of the law. The execution of fuch laws
comes in only in the fecond place, and is
to be confidered merely as the remedy, which
is to be applied, when the bare declaration
of the law is not effectual to procure obedience. But, if the laws themfelves are good,
it is univerfally allowed that, when they are
broken, the execution of them ought to follow. When laws, therefore, are faid to
ftand in terrorem ONLY, or without any view
to the infliction of the penalty appointed
by them, the very form of the expreffion
implies, that there are fome circumftances
annexed to them which render the execution
of them unfit. To fuppofe of any laws, that
they are not fit to be executed, is giving,
at beft, but a very unfavourable, difhonour-
able reprefentation of them ; and the farther
we enter into the grounds of the fuppofition,
the more unfavourable to the credit of fuch
laws it will appear. For why are they not
fit to be executed ? If it is becaufe they
are calculated to produce more evil than
good.

good, they are bad laws in point of policy.
—But if it is ·becaufe they· are unjuft, in
refpect to their end, or the means by which
they direct that end to be purfued, they are
bad in point of confcience; and no competent
caufe can be affigned for retaining them.
They cannot,- as Dr. Furneaux has· juftly
obferved,ª " be confidered as the offspring
" of political wifdom, fo much as of an
" arbitrary and tyrannical difpofition." And,
as they were enacted upon indefenfible principles; fo no merely poffible conveniencies,
which may be imagined to refult from them,
are weighty enough to fhew that it is .right
to permit them to remain, were the reality
of fuch conveniencies to be admitted.   But
in fact, the argument drawn from them is
as deftitute of foundation, as it is void of
ftrength; and, inftead of fortifying the credit
of fuch laws, tends rather to weaken it.

Let the notion of laws, kept up merely in
TERROREM, be ftrictly adhered to, and it will
be evident, to fay the gentleft things of
them, that they muft be of little or no ufe.
If any doubt can arife concerning this, it
muft proceed from hence, that fome laws
may be inadvertently comprehended under
this denomination, only becaufe it is but
feldom that occafions happen to require the
execution of them; but this is departing from
the

ª Letters to Sir William Blackftone, 2d ed. p. 122.

the fignification of the phrafe, as it is applied in the cafe under confideration. Inftances of perfons fuffering for treafon and
rebellion are, in general, but rare, and bear
no proportion to the number of thofe, who
fuffer on other accounts; and yet no one, it
is prefumed, imagines, for this reafon, that
the laws againft thofe offences, are laws
merely in terrorem. The laws concerned in
the prefent debate, are laws, the execution
of which is laid afide, though the objects,
againft which they are directed, are continually exifting. They are laws which are virtually condemned, by a general difapprobation
of the execution of them, as improper to be
renewed. And, when it is afked, of what advantage it can be to retain fuch laws as thefe ;
which are not only fallen into neglect, but,
which the very advocates for their continuance confefs ought to be left in this
neglected ftate ; the queftion, thus ftated,
carries its own anfwer with it : and a moderate fhare of attention to the very terms
of it will fatisfy us, that their continuance
can be of no advantage. When the dread
of a law ceafes, all the efficacy of the law
ceafes with it. When the execution of the
law is entirely thrown afide, efpecially when
it is by common confent exploded ; (which
in the cafe here argued it is) the dread of
the law foon comes to an end. For it is

the

the execution, which fupports the terror, gives it all its permanence, vigour and effect; and when that is given up, all the practical authority of the law is given up alfo: and all their ufe, upon fuppofition that it were poffible for them ever to be of any fervice, is deftroyed.

But the ufeleffnefs of keeping fuch laws in force is the leaft objection to it: the confequences of it may be highly pernicious. Bad laws may be fuffered to fleep for a feafon, and, while they remain in this dormant ftate, may be treated as very harmlefs, inoffenfive things. But the power of oppreffing, by their means, abides;—this power, by fome combination of unhappy circumftances, may be awakened into action; and, perhaps, among the whole body of obnoxious penal laws, there are none, which are more likely to be moft grofsly perverted, and be made the inftruments of the moft infupportable evils, than thofe, which have been for a time difcarded, and afterwards refumed for execution. For what is it, which moft commonly brings them into this difgrace, but a conviction that they are yokes too heavy to be endured? What, but a conviction that they are inconfiftent with the laws of reafon and humanity; that to enforce them is repugnant to the principles of natural and political juftice; and would be equally oppofite to

b the

the fafety of individuals, and the tranquillity
of the publick ?   The execution of fuch laws
can never be fuppofed to be revived, but
from bad views and difpofitions : and from
this confideration, alone, it is eafy to forefee,
of what innumerable mifchiefs they may become the occafion.   Regard to the laws will
be the pretended reafon, for the profecutions
commenced upon them ; but the advancement of fome finifter defign will be the
real one.   Private intereft, pique, revenge,
and other bafe and unworthy principles, will
be fheltered under the cover of what, in fuch
feafons, would be ftiled juftice, order, and
the fupport of authority ; and a counterfeit
zeal for the welfare of the ftate, become a
cloak for every malicious and fhameful inclination, by which we can fuppofe the worft
of men to be prompted.   Nor are thefe only
arbitrary affertions, which deferve to be
treated as unworthy of regard.   All, who
are acquainted with hiftory, well know, that
fome of the worft acts of injuftice, which
are recorded in it, have been committed under the fanction of OBSOLETE LAWS; that
is (if it be poffible for any of my readers,
to want fuch an explanation) laws grown
into difufe, though fupinely fuffered to continue in force; and which, if they were remembered to be laws at all, were confidered

as

as laws, which were permitted to retain that name in TERROREM only.

But if we afcend to the primary princi- ples, to which all political regulations ought to be adjufted, we fhall be furnifhed with frefh evidence, that no laws, founded upon injuftice, let the execution of them be ever fo little intended, or expected, are capable of a folid vindication. Laws ought to guard againft oppreffion, from whatever quarter it is apprehended. — Such laws as thefe, give power to opprefs; incorporate incroachments upon the rights of men into the conftitu- tion; and arm thofe, who are difpofed to violate the peace of others, with the force of publick authority. They are fo far from being proper means of preferving the pub- lick tranquillity, that they are the moft im- proper ones, which can be chofen for that purpofe. For, in their natural operation, they are adapted only to create diftrefs and confufion: and, if it be poffible for any par- ticular circumftances to arife, in which fome momentary convenience may refult from them; there are other methods, by which the evils, (which it is pretended they may be of ufe to check,) may be remedied with in- comparably greater efficacy, fafety and ho- nour. If the apprehended evils are, in rea- lity, proper objects of punifhment by the civil magiftrate, furely the regular, obvious

courfe

courfe to be purfued, is to eftablifh proper
laws againft them: and not to think of fuppreffing them by making or fupporting laws,
which decree penalties againft what no human power has a right to punifh; which directly forbid what, it is allowed, ought not
to be forbidden; and while they, perhaps,
make no mention of what is really an offence againft the obligations of good fubjects,
condemn only that, which the judgment of
men has no authority to reftrain. Laws directed againft thofe actions, which fall properly under their cognizance; (in which the
nature of the offence is clearly defined, and
the fanctions of them duly proportioned to
the offences which they prohibit) will generally have their influence confined within
its proper limits. The terrors of them will
be aimed at their original and juft object;
and there is, comparatively, but little dan-
ger of their being abufed. But to have recourfe to laws, intended to prevent one thing,
to reftrain another, which is totally diftinct
from it, and has, perhaps, no probable, and
certainly no neceffary connexion with it; and
to ordain penalties, in cafes in which they can
never be juft, merely becaufe it is poffible,
that they may, by chance, be employed in
cafes where punifhments may be juft; (that
is, in other words, to make the innocent
directly obnoxious to fufferings, merely for

the

the fake of accidentally reaching the guilty ;)
is giving fcope to an endlefs variety of op-
preffions. For? the execution of laws, which
are thus made ufe of, being directed, not by
any rule arifing from the laws themfelves, but
by the inclination of thofe, who call in their
force, will always be arbitrary in their application : and the confequence of this is,
that they will always be liable to be perverted
into fome of the worft engines of tyranny ;
engines, againft which no caution is able to
guard, and by which perfons, the moft un-
queftionably harmlefs, and without rebuke,
may be given up to be harraffed by every
man, who has either an intereft to ferve,
or a paffion to gratify, by difturbing them.
And is this an expedient, to which it can
ever be neceffary to the fafety, or fuitable
to the dignity, of a well ordered ftate, to
have recourfe ? It appears, on the contrary,
to be fuch a folecifm in government, and fo
inconfiftent with all political wifdom, that,
without the ftrongeft evidence, it is not to
be imputed to any fet of legiflators whatfoever. And, indeed, to urge it in the cafe
before us feems to be only an after thought,
to give fome countenance to the continuance
of laws, for the making of which it is not
pretended, that any good plea can be offered.
This was plainly not the original light, in
which they were confidered by the authors

of

of them, who sufficiently shewed themselves in earneft for the execution of them; though the better judgment, and better spirit of the prefent times, has utterly condemned them.

When laws are allowed to be indefenfible, the natural expectation, from fuch a conceffion, is, that thofe, who acknowledge this, should approve of giving them up. That the penal laws, from which the diffenters requefted a farther exemption, are of this kind, feems to be confeffed; and every argument againft keeping up unjuft laws, in terrorem, in general, muft be acknowledged to conclude againft them in particular; and yet, ftrange as it may feem, a neceffity is pleaded for their continuing in force, to keep the diffenters in awe. But let it be allowed to afk, whence this neceffity arifes? Or againft what is it that all thefe terrors are pointed? It furely cannot be againft attempts to hurt the eftablifhment by force. Were there no fuch laws as thofe, which we are confidering, in being; the laws, by which every man, and every body of men, are protected in the enjoyment of their properties and priviledges, would be an ample fecurity againft all fuch encroachments. The continuance of thefe laws cannot, again, be thought neceffary, from a defire to deter the diffenters from writing and fpeaking in defence of their religious principles and practices. For the diffenters to

admit

admit this thought, would be to impute to
their brethren of the eſtabliſhment a diſtruſt
of their cauſe, with a ſuſpicion of which, they
might be juſtly diſpleaſed; and to charge
them with an inclination to ſubſtitute force
inſtead of argument, which they would diſ-
claim with indignation. To ſuppoſe theſe
laws are retained from an apprehenſion, that
the doctrines of the church could not ſubſiſt without them, would be a reflection upon
the articles of it, which the friends to them
would have reaſon to reſent. Truth wants
nothing but an impartial hearing. — The
way to promote the intereſt of it is to permit the judgments of men to determine freely, by the evidence which appears before
them, unbiaſſed by the terrors of this world;
and it can never be to the honour of any
cauſe, to think it wants any of theſe aids
to ſupport it, or redound to the praiſe of its
advocates to depend upon them. And yet,
againſt what other contingencies thoſe, who
contend for keeping up the terror of theſe
laws, can think it neceſſary to maintain ſuch
a powerful guard, it is not eaſy to conceive.
The apprehenſions of indecency and petu-
lance, on the part of the diſſenters, need
give them no pain; — Theſe are faults which,
wherever they are found, furniſh the beſt
antidotes againſt themſelves, and never fail to
diſcredit the cauſe of thoſe, who have ſo little
                                    judgment

judgment and temper as to give way to them.
And were these excesses to prevail much more
frequently, and in a higher degree, than can be
reasonably supposed; yet to desire to have a
person lie at the mercy of cruel and unjust
laws, and be subject to ruin, merely because
in the warmth of a controversy, he has lost
his caution, has something in it, which a
man of true greatness of mind will abhor;
and one, who has a just reverence for his
own reputation, will be extremely backward
to acknowledge.

Hitherto the propriety of suffering the penal statutes against dissenters, to hold the
place in our laws, which is still left to them
by the act of Toleration, has been considered
as it rests upon the general expedience of
keeping them up as laws in terrorem only.
But, besides the objections, which have already been urged against them, upon this
footing; the antagonists of the dissenters, in
this case, have embarrassed themselves with
new difficulties; and, by endeavouring to
mollify the severity of that side of the question, which they defend, have taken away
the force of all the arguments, by which
they attempt to vindicate it.   To reconcile
the dissenters to their disappointment, they
have been told, that all their fears are vi-
sionary, that they may make themselves perfectly

fectly easy, [b] " the state will not attend to
" their preaching, and the church are en-
" gaged in labours of their own. " Let
this, for the present, be granted. The question still returns, (and returns with additional
force :) for what reason, then, are those re-
licks of persecution, which are yet contained in the laws against dissenters, so tenaci-
ously held fast ? Or on what account is a
legal assurance of that safety, which it is
acknowledged the dissenting ministers ought
to enjoy, and which they are so confidently
told they will enjoy, deemed so improper ?
To attempt, in any form, to vindicate the
perpetuating of laws confessedly bad, merely for the sake of striking terror, is attempting an arduous task. But to represent these
laws as harmless, because no use will ever
be made of them ; and, at the same time,
speak of the repeal of them as a risk not
to be run, is surely very peculiar. It is, if
the expression will be pardoned, a self-de-
structive mode of reasoning, which saps the
very foundation, upon which it appears to
stand ; and brings those, who adopt it, into
the midst of contradictions. If, as the author of the letter to the dissenting ministers
tells them, [c] all that part of the law, by
which they think themselves aggrieved, " is
" now as dead, as if the whole were ob-

c

" solete ;

---

[b] Letter, p. 17.   [c] Ibid. p. 37.

" folete ; " where is the terror it is fuppofed to contain ? Or what is become of
that fecurity, which it is fuppofed to give
to church and ftate ? If thefe laws, on the
other hand, are referved, becaufe occafions
may call for their execution; from whence
can the diffenting minifters derive that entire fatisfaction, in their prefent circumftances, which is recommended to them ? If the
execution of thefe laws is to ceafe for ever,
where would be the harm of a law for
quieting the minds of the diffenters, by giving them a proper, real fecurity from thofe
laws, which difturb them ? But, if thofe
may yet be the inftruments of oppreffion,
and the apprehenfion of this may juftly make
the diffenters uneafy; why fhould they be
cenfured as raifing a [needlefs] ferment [d] by
their application ? Or with what equity can
they be blamed, as indulging unreafonable
jealoufies, when the very reafons affigned for
denying their petition, have fuch an apparent
tendency to keep their apprehenfions awake ?
When they think, indeed, of the liberal fentiments and exemplary moderation, which reflect
fo much honour on the members of the eftablifhment, their fears vanifh. But the fame
excellent fpirit, which dwells in thefe valuable
perfons, may not defcend to others. If it
fhould, yet, as our laws now ftand, it is
not

[d] Letter, p. 22.

not in the power of thofe, who may have
the beft inclination to it, to infure the fafety
of the diffenters from the dangers, to which
they are expofed : and, when thefe things are
candidly confidered, it cannot be juftly
thought ftrange, if they are ftill defirous to
enjoy the advantage of legal fafety ; and be
completely affured of the unmolefted exercife
of thofe rights of human nature, which, as a
very able writer has happily expreffed it, [e]
" ought to have every protection and ground
" of fecurity, which law and the policy of
" free ftates can give them."

How far the cafe of the diffenters is intitled to the benefit of this valuable protection, they muft leave to the judgment
of the legiflature; to which their petition
is again, with all deference and humility,
fubmitted. With thefe difpofitions, they
hope every ftep, which they take, will
be found to be conducted; and as they are
fatisfied, that making an application for the
removal of what they have efteemed a grievance, will never be condemned by thofe
great affemblies, to which they look up; fo
they are willing to believe, that, if any of
their fellow fubjects have been inclinable to
cenfure them for this reafon, it will, upon
further confideration appear, that they have
been

[e] Dr. Furneaux's preface to the 1ft edit. of his
letters, &c. p. 17. 2d edit.

been censured without cause; and that they are
liable to no imputation of having made any
request, which it would be unfit for the most
dutiful subjects to present, or inconsistent with
the honour of government to grant.   To
borrow the words of a confessedly competent
judge of this matter; " Sapientissimi etiam
" legislatores non omnia viderunt, quæ rei-
" publicæ utilia aut noxia esse possunt; &
" plerumque progressu temporis accidit, ut
" morum, personarum, aut rerum mutatio,
" ALIA planê sanciri desideret.   Sollemnis
" illa jurisconsultorum romanorum formula,
" DURUM, SED ITA SCRIPTA LEX EST; illud
" inquam, tamdiu valere debet, quamdiu
" sine graviori incommodo, quod durum est,
" aut tolli, aut emolliri non potest; SED UBI
" PRIMUM DATA EST OCCASIO, eo redeat lex
" iniqua, unde malum pedem tulerat; nulla
" idonea causa est, quare summæ potestates
" auctoritate sua illam tueri porro pergant." [f]

[f] Barbeyrac. orat. inaugural. de dignitate, et uti-
litate, juris, ac Histor. p 17. Droit de la nature,
& des Genev. edit. Amsterd. 1712. tom ii. a la fin.

An

An ENQUIRY, &c.

THE worthy and refpectable Dr.
Law, [a] fpeaking of the common
difpofition to extol the former
times at the expence of the prefent, mentions two circumftances, among
others, in which the latter are greatly pre-
ferable. One is, " that we have certain
" virtues now in greater perfection ; parti-
" cularly, more of true charity, or univerfal
" benevolence, than ever fince the time of
" primitive chriftianity : " [b] and the other,
" that we live under the mildeft, moft in-
" dulgent of all Governments ; and enjoy the
" bleffing of liberty in that perfection, which
" has been unknown to former ages, and
" is fo ftill to moft other nations." [c] The
truth of the obfervation is granted. But
fhould it be inferred from hence, that the

B   fpirit

---

[a] The prefent Bifhop of *Carlifle*. [b] Confiderations on
Religion, Part III. p. 243. Ed. 1765. [c] p. 259, 260.

spirit of the times, and the state of our laws are brought to such a degree of perfection, as to need no farther improvement, it would be an error; an error, which would need correction equally with that, which this candid writer makes it his business to rectify. These are points, indeed, which are never to be taken for granted in the most advantageous situation, in which we can suppose ourselves to be placed. Sober enquiries whether there are not still some mistakes to be corrected; some remains of the injudicious appointments of the seasons of comparative ignorance, which it would be both just and wise to remove; and some defects, which greatly need to be supplied; are always worthy of attention. Such an enquiry into the state of religious liberty among ourselves is here attempted; and the author sincerely regrets that there should be such weighty reasons for his entering upon it, as he apprehends there are. It appears, indeed, to be a subject very far from being universally seen in its true light. Whether any thing, which is here offered, may contribute to lead persons to juster apprehensions of it, must be left to the judgment of others. This can be affirmed with great truth that, whatever is said, proceeds only from a sincere concern to clear up the rights of conscience more completely, and

promote

promote the exemption of it from every unwarrantable impofition; which has a much clofer connection with the intereft of religion, and virtue, than is generally imagined. . Whatever therefore may be the fate of his reafonings, the author hopes the freedom, which he takes of laying his fentiments before the world, will not be cenfured.

In order to difcover the genuine Principles of Toleration, it is neceffary to look back to the original liberties of mankind : and that, antecedently to the confideration of their being formed into civil focieties, there are certain rights belonging to them, independent of all human grant, not derived from any compact, and which are, therefore to be acknowledged as the rights of human nature, it is prefumed will not be called into queftion. That a right to judge for themfelves in points of religion, is, in thefe circumftances, one of thefe rights, muft be equally evident; and to attempt a formal proof of it, is needlefs. It is a principle, in reality, fo obvioufly true, and reafonable, as to be fcarcely liable to contradiction, or capable of illuftration. But the neceffary confequences of this UNIVERSAL right of men may deferve more particular attention; for, while it authorizes every individual to claim the exercife of this priviledge to

himfelf,

himfelf, it obliges him to allow it, in the very fame extent, to all about him; and eftablifhes one uniform regulation for his behaviour towards others, and their behaviour towards him. It is evident, for inftance, that no apprehenfions of the truth, and certainty of any perfon's religious fentiments, can juftify him in attempting to impofe them on his neighbour : for the fame right of judgment, which any ONE can claim, belongs, on the fame principle, equally to ALL, and ought to be equally facred, and inviolable in all; and no reafon can be alledged by him for taking the religious liberty of others from them, but what will, at the fame time, equally deftroy his own title to it. It can juftify no man in breaking in upon the peace, property, or enjoyments of others. They hold their claim to be unmolefted in all thefe refpects, by the fame tenure, by which he holds his : and it is impoffible for him to fet it afide, in their cafe, without virtually renouncing it in his own. The injuftice of all fuch encroachments upon HIM from OTHERS follows from the fame principle, with the fame force of evidence; and, if any attempt towards them fhould be made, common fenfe and equity muft condemn and oppofe it. In fhort, whatever apprehenfions fome perfons, not ufed to think upon the fubject, may en-

tertain

tertain, that claiming fuch a.liberty of judgment in religion for ourfelves might open
a door to invafions of the rights of others;
nothing is plainer, than that it gives not the
leaft real countenance to them. It places the
ftrongeft guard againft them, and may fafely be adopted in all its juft confequences.
Whether this claim is weakened by men's
entering into civil fociety, is the next thing
to be confidered.

The great end of government is to protect the fubjects of it from the injuries, to
which they were expofed in a ftate of nature. Thefe injuries may be divided into
internal and external; or thofe to which perfons, who by any natural tie, or accidental
circumftance are connected together, are obnoxious from each other; and thofe, to which
they are liable from any perfons, or number
of perfons, not thus connected with them.
This latter clafs of injuries is here out of
the queftion, and only thofe of the former
come under confideration. Now all injuries
imply, in the very notion of them, fome
rights, of which they are violations; all the
care, which is taken to guard againft the violation of thefe rights, is an acknowledgment
of the reality and importance of them: and,
if the primary and leading view of government be, as it has juft been ftated, to prevent or reftrain thofe injuries, to which men
were

were expofed for want of its protection; it is evidently implied, that, when they enter into civil fociety, they carry thefe rights with them;—that they continue to retain them;—and that, inftead of fuppofing them-felves to be deprived of them, the very de-fign, with which they put themfelves under the authority of government, is to SECURE them the more firmly. I am very fenfible, that this matter is, commonly, otherwife ap-prehended. It is fuppofed by many, that, when men enter into civil focieties, they give up their liberties; furrender their rights into the hands of the ruling powers; and become entirely dependent, for the enjoyment of any part of them, on the pleafure of their fu-periors. That this is in fact the general con-fequence of their living in fociety, there can be no doubt. But it is not by attending only to the PRACTICE of Governors, and to the extent of that mere force and power which is fuppofed in the abftract notion of fupremacy, to be annexed to their office; it is not, I fay, by appealing to thefe confiderations, that fuch queftions, as this before us, are to be determined; but by entering into the great defign of that power, and attending to the exprefs, or implied conditions, upon which it is committed to them, and the meafures, by which the exercife of it is to be adjufted. ——It is certain, again, that reftraint is, in

fome

some degree, effential to the very being of
fubjection to government. Wherever it is
eftablifhed, there muft be fome common laws,
by which thofe, who live under it, muft agree
to be controuled. There muft be fome common ruler invefted with authority, and armed
with power, to enforce the obfervation of thofe
laws. The members of the fociety muft
confent to leave to the magiftrate the deter-
mination of thofe civil difputes, which they
either cannot, or do not, compromife between
themfelves; and the punifhment of thofe violations of their rights, for which, if there
were no fuch perfon impowered to redrefs
their wrongs, they muft have done themfelves
juftice. In confequence of this they confent
to defift from thofe forcible methods of aven-
ging the injuries, which are offered them, to
which, in a ftate of independence on government, all men have an equal right; and
to have recourfe to thofe methods of relief,
which are appointed by the laws of the fociety to which they belong. But all this is
far, very far, from amounting to an abfolute
divefting themfelves of all thofe rights, which
they enjoyed antecedently to their forming
themfelves into fuch communities. It is, on
the contrary, raifing up perfons to be the
defenders of them, and entrufting the prefervation of them to COMMON GUARDIANS, by
whofe intervention, it is prefumed, they will
be

be more vigorously asserted, and more effectually protected, than it is possible they
should be in a state, where there is no common umpire to check the evils of oppression
on the one hand, and restrain the no less
formidable evils of immoderate resentment
on the other. And if we only give ourselves
leave to reflect a little on the nature of those
rights, the exercise of which they transfer
to the magistrate, this will make the point
I am illustrating yet clearer.

For what are the rights which men give up
to government ? Not those, which may most
properly be stiled the primary rights of human
nature. Not the right, which every innocent
man has, to live undisturbed, enjoy the advantages, which he justly possesses, and be
left to his freedom in all things, not injurious
to his fellow creatures ; but the consequen-
tial, though equally real and certain right,
which, where men are not subject to government, every person has to take the assertion
of all his rights into his own hands, and
correct the infringers of them, by the infliction of such pains, or the use of such
other methods of deterring the authors of
the wrong, as reason shall warrant for his
future security. And after all, if we speak
precisely, even THESE rights are not absolutely
extinguished and utterly lost, but suspended
by such limitations, as the order and well-
being

being of fociety require, and fo long as the fuccours of government fhall be effectual; as is evident from hence, that many cafes may be fuppofed, and are frequently occurring, even under the beft regulated governments, in which the ufe of force for our own prefervation is not efteemed culpable, even in a political fenfe. For it is granted, I think by all, who have been moft valued for their judgment in thefe fubjects, that wherever the aid of the fociety is too diftant to prevent the injury, and the evil, which, if we neglect to fecure ourfelves, will be brought upon us, is of fuch a nature as to be irreparable by any redrefs which government can give; there all the original rights of felf-defence return, and it is warrantable to repel force by force.[d] Inquifition indeed always is, and always ought to be made in thefe cafes, to determine whether fuch neceffity exifted: but, if it is found to have been real, and urgent, and the impending evil was irreparable, and unavoidable by any other method; the felf-defence is allowed, even though it proved fatal to the aggreffor.[e] From all which it appears, that the primary rights of liberty, fafety, and protection from oppreffion

C ftill

---

[d] Puffendorff, L. ii. c. 5. §. 7, 8. per Barbeyrac. Grot. J. B. & P. L. ii. c. i. §. 3—7. Edit. Barbeyrac.

[e] Sir William Blackftone's Commentaries, vol. i. p. 130. 2d Edit.

ftill fubfift in their full vigour. To fuppofe
them abandoned, renounced and annihilated,
or that government can have any right to
deftroy them, is afcribing to it a right to
defeat the very end, for which it is eftablifhed, and betray the truft repofed in it. It is
indeed totally inverting the principle, upon
which the power of rulers ftands, and by
which the acts of it ought to be guided. ——
Man was not made for government, but
government for man; and the great object,
to which all the operations of it fhould be
directed, is to guard, as much as poffible,
the equal, impartial, eafe and freedom of all
the fubjects of it. And if it fhould be
thought by any that thefe expreffions are too
ftrong, the author is perfuaded they will alter
their opinion, upon their perufal of the following excellent paffage from Sir William
Blackftone's valuable Commentaries on the
Laws of England. It is needlefs to make an
apology for the length of the quotation : my
readers cannot wonder that I fhould embrace
the opportunity of availing myfelf of fuch a
refpectable authority ; and, whether they have
already perufed it or not, will dwell upon it
with pleafure.

" The principal aim of fociety," fays this
judicious writer, ' " is to protect individuals
" in the enjoyment of thofe abfolute rights,
" which

' Comment. Vol. i. p. 124—126.

" which were vefted in them by the immu-
" table laws of nature, but which could not
" be preferved in peace, without that mutual
" affiftance and intercourfe, which is gained
" by the inftitution of friendly and focial com-
" munities. — Hence it follows, that the firft
" and primary end of human laws, is to main-
" tain and regulate thefe abfolute rights of
" individuals. Such rights as are focial, and
" relative, refult from, and are pofterior to
" the formation of ftates and focieties; fo
" that to maintain and regulate thefe is clear-
" ly a fubfequent confideration. And there-
" fore the principal view of human laws is,
" or always ought to be, to explain, protect
" and enforce fuch rights as are abfolute,
" which in themfelves are few and fimple;
" and then fuch rights as are relative, which,
" arifing from a variety of connexions, will be
" far more numerous and more complicated.
" — The abfolute rights of man, (he goes on
" to obferve a few lines after,) confidered as
" a free agent, endowed with difcernment to
" know good from evil, and with power of
" chufing thofe meafures, which appear to
" him to be moft defirable, are ufually fum-
" med up in one general appellation, and
" denominated the natural liberty of man-
" kind. This natural liberty confifts proper-
" ly, in a power of acting as one thinks fit,
" without any reftraint or controul; unlefs

　　　　　　" by

" by the law of nature ; being a right inhe-
" rent in us by birth; and one of the gifts
" of God to man at his creation, when he
" endued him with the faculty of free will.
" But every man when he enters into fociety
" gives up a part of his natural liberty as
" the price of fo valuable a purchafe ; and,
" in confideration of receiving the advan-
" tages of mutual commerce, obliges himfelf
" to conform to thofe laws, which the commu-
" nity has thought proper to eftablifh.   And
" this fpecies of legal obedience and confor-
" mity is infinitely more defirable than that
" wild and favage liberty, which is facrificed
" to obtain it.   For no man that confiders
" a moment, would wifh to retain the ab-
" folute and uncontrouled power of doing
" whatever he pleafes ; the confequence of
" which is, that every other man would alfo
" have the fame power ; and then there would
" be no fecurity to individuals in any of
" the enjoyments of life.   Political, there-
" fore, or civil, liberty, which is that of a
" member of fociety, is no other than na-
" tural liberty, fo far reftrained by human
" laws (AND NO FARTHER) as is ne-
" ceffary and expedient for the general ad-
" vantage of the publick.   Hence we may
" collect that the law, which reftrains a man
" from doing mifchief to his fellow citizens,
" though it diminifhes the natural, increafes
                                                    " the

" the civil liberty of mankind : but every
" wanton and caufelefs reftraint of the will
" of the fubject, whether practifed by a mo-
" narch, a nobility, or a popular affembly,
" is a degree of tyranny. Nay, that even
" LAWS themfelves, whether made with or
" without our confent, if they regulate and
" conftrain our conduct in matters of mere
" indifference, without any good end in view,
" are laws deftructive of liberty; whereas,
" if any publick advantage can arife from
" obferving fuch precepts, the controul of our
" private inclinations, in one or two particu-
" lar points, will conduce to preferve our ge-
" neral freedom, in others of more importance,
" by fupporting that ftate of fociety, which
" can alone fecure our independency. Thus
" the ftatute of King Edward IV. which
" forbad the fine gentlemen of thofe times
" (under the degree of a lord) to wear pikes
" upon their fhoes or boots of more than
" two inches in length, was a law that fa-
" voured of oppreffion ; becaufe, however
" ridiculous the fafhion then in ufe might ap-
" pear, the reftraining it by pecuniary penalties
" could ferve no purpofe of common utility.
" But the ftatute of King Charles II. which
" prefcribes a thing feemingly as indifferent,
" viz. a drefs for the dead, who are all or-
" dered to be buried in woollen, is a law
" confiftent with public liberty ; for it en-
" courages

" courages the ftaple trade, on which, in
" great meafure, depends the univerfal good
" of the nation. So that laws, when pru-
" dently framed, are by no means fubverfive
" but rather introductive of liberty; for, (as
" Mr. Locke has well obferved) where there
" is no law there is no freedom. But then,
" on the other hand, that conftitution or
" frame of government, that fyftem of laws,
" is alone calculated to maintain civil liberty,
" which leaves the fubject ENTIRE MASTER
" OF HIS OWN CONDUCT, EXCEPT IN THOSE
" POINTS WHEREIN THE PUBLIC GOOD RE-
" QUIRES SOME DIRECTION OR RESTRAINT."
Thus far this able writer. Whether there
be any thing in the letter, or fpirit of our
laws, contrary to thefe noble declarations, is
a queftion, which needs not create the leaft
uneafinefs to the author of this valuable performance. He could report the laws no
otherwife than he found them. If there
fhould be any fuch inconfiftency, it cannot in
the leaft invalidate the certainty, and weight
of the truths, which he has here delivered.
They hold, indeed, the rank of AXIOMS in
the doctrine of government, carry their own
evidence with them, and merit the thanks
of all, who are cordially attached to the
caufe of liberty, and concerned for the advancement of the welfare of fociety.

Now

Now, of all the rights inherent in human nature, that of thinking for ourfelves, and following the conviction of our own judgments in relation to the object of our faith, worfhip, and religious obedience, is the moft facred, inconteftable, and, in every view of it, intitled to the moft careful protection. It is, in the nature of it, the moft important to every Being capable of moral obligation. It is the moft effential to our peace, and that which every good man will be moft tenderly concerned to have fecured to him. If therefore, the prefervation of the great natural and abfolute rights of men be one of the chief, I fhould, perhaps, rather have faid the very FIRST, of all the intentions, with which civil focieties are inftituted, and the rulers of them invefted with power; what is the confequence from thefe premifes? Muft it not be this, that, in all governments, the rights of conficence fhould have a principal place affigned them in the care of thofe, to whom the protection of their fellow creatures is committed? If the fecuring of equal, impartial liberty in all thofe inftances of it, in which it is not injurious to others, be fo much the object of every equitable, wife, and well conftituted fyftem of laws, that all needlefs encroachments upon it are deviations from the fpirit, which ought to be diffufed through all laws, and impair the very benefit, which
they

they ought to confirm; can it be fuppofed that the rights of confcience ought not to be guarded from violation? To take for granted a renunciation of thefe rights, when men enter into fociety, is, of all prefumptions, the moft groundlefs. They are the laft rights, which men can ever be imagined to give up to be modelled at the pleafure of others; nor is there any one principle connected with their fubmiffion to governors in other refpects, from which fuch an inference can be deduced. Does it follow, that, becaufe the magiftrate is entrufted with authority to decide difputes between us and our fellow citizens concerning property, he is authorized alfo to determine points, which lie only between God and our own confciences? Becaufe it is allowed to be his office to guard the peace of his fubjects, and to inflict punifhments for this purpofe on thofe, who unjuftly difturb it; is it to be taken for granted, that he is to dictate to them what rule of faith they fhall adopt, and in what manner they are to worfhip the Deity, when it is allowed on all hands, that of thefe things the will of God is the only rule, and that no worfhip can be acceptable to him, but what is accompanied with the fincere conviction of him who offers it? Nay, there is no prefumption in advancing a ftep further, and afferting that fuch is the nature of this right;

and

and in this refpect, it ftands upon a foundation peculiar to itfelf, and is diftinguifhed from every other right, that it cannot be given up. Property may be refigned, transferred, or fubmitted to the regulation of others. — A man may in many inftances relinquifh his eafe, and fubject himfelf to inconveniences, and, in fo doing, act not only an innocent but a laudable part.—Cafes may occur, in which a man may facrifice life itfelf, and the facrifice may merit the higheft applaufe. But his CONSCIENCE, he cannot refign. To prove all things, and hold faft that, which is good, is not only a privilege but a duty ; an obligation laid upon him, by the very nature of religion and virtue, and from which he cannot difcharge himfelf without departing from the principles of both. It muft always remain entire to him ; nor, while the principles of the moft reafonable liberty are allowed to fubfift in their due extent, can any attempt be confiftently made to take it from him.

There is no difficulty in difcerning, that while I am fpeaking in this manner, an objection will offer itfelf to the reader ; and that it will be fuppofed, that my own reafoning may be retorted againft me. The more important confcience is reprefented, the more, it will be faid, it falls under the infpection of the magiftrate. To exempt it thus from

D   hi..

his jurifdiction will be thought laying a
foundation for excluding him, by degrees,
from taking that care of the fafety of his
fubjects, which is confeffed to be a part of
his office. Religion, it will be urged, may
be made a plea for any thing; and, if governors muft never interpofe to reftrain it,
there is no enormity but what will pafs
unpunifhed. But thefe objections arife entirely from imperfect views of the principle,
which is here afferted. To contend for a
right to think for themfelves in fome, and
deny it to others, might indeed be chargeable with thefe confequences. But to contend for this, as a right to which EVERY
INDIVIDUAL has a claim equally valid and
clear, never can be juftly liable to fuch an
imputation. For a man firft to own, that
not only he, but all around him have an
indifputable right, the very fame right with
himfelf, to be guided by their own confciences in religion, (and let it be remembered, it is thus the matter has all along
been ftated) for a man to allow this, I fay,
and yet make his perfuafion a pretence for
taking that liberty from them, is a contradiction fo grofs and palpable, that it is fcarcely
conceivable a perfon in poffeffion of his
underftanding can fall into it. Were a
perfon to be fuppofed capable of this ex-
travagance, every one would inftantly difcern

cern that the very principle, upon which he pretends to act, condemns him. Were it again fuppofed, that the magiftrate was to guard a part of his fubjects only in the rights of confcience, it might be poffible for that favourite part to make it a cover for violating the peace and fafety of others with impunity : but let this protection be granted impartially to all of them, and no fuch confequences can take place. For protection confifts in the prevention or fuppreffion of injuries; and while this is allowed to be the office and duty of the magiftrate, the duty, which he is to difcharge equally to every one under his care, he will always have an unqueftionable right, as the guardian of the whole community, whenever fuch mifdemeanors are committed, to animadvert upon the authors of them. Nor is maintaining this at all repugnant to the general principles here afferted. For it is not in a religious, but political view, that fuch diforders come under his cognizance. It is not as offences againft God, but as hurtful to the community, and breaches of the peace that he punifhes them. [g] Where this is not violated

---

[g] What is obferved above is not very different from what has been often faid; but there is one thing more to be confidered here, which, though it muft have occurred to every thinking perfon, I do not remember

lated, the right of following their own convictions in religion without being molested for it, continues : the more facred, important, and valuable it is; (and valuable it muft be allowed to be to the advancement of truth, the real intereft of fociety, and the

remember to have feen fo diftin&ly mentioned as, perhaps, it ought to have been, viz. that the cafes, in which the magiftrate has a right thus to interpofe, are the very fame, in which perfons out of civil fociety would have a right to defend themfelves. Should a man, in the ftate of nature, be fo weak or fo wicked as, from a real, or pretended, plea of confcience, to opprefs, defraud, or in any refpe& mifufe another, every individual thus injured would be juftified in punifhing, or (if that word fhould be thought improper, where no government is fuppofed to exift) in reftraining the tranfgreffor by force. His neighbours might lawfully affift him, or, if they thought it neceffary, enter into a confederacy to defend themfelves againft all fuch attempts upon their common fecurity. This right, indeed, lodged in the hand of the magiftrate, will, in all probability, be much more equitably and effectually exerted, than by fingle, independent perfons : but the end of fuch an exertion of it is precifely the fame, the nature of the occafions upon which he is to exercife this power is not changed, nor is the leaft right to ufe force in matters of confcience, as fuch, acquired by him in confequence of his having fuch a truft repofed in him. For his right to fupport his authority in the juft execution of his office neither enlarges, or contracts, the bounds of any part of the office itfelf; the extent of which is always to be determined by the extent of thofe rights, for the defence of which he was invefted with his dignity.

the caufe of pure and undefiled religion)
the more effectually it fhould be guarded
from every encroachment upon it: and by
this general rule, the real, genuine principles
of Toleration are to be determined.

Let what has been obferved then be applied to this purpofe. — And we may collect
from it in what light Toleration in general
ought to be confidered. There is room to
think, (more room than was till of late apprehended) that it is confidered by many as
a matter of mere grace or favour, which
government has a right to withhold, grant,
abridge, or refume at pleafure. But, if the
arguments, which have been advanced, are
conclufive, it ftands on a totally different
foundation. It is the acknowledgment and
confirmation of a right; not one of thofe
adventitious rights, which are fubfequent to
the eftablifhment of civil focieties, and arife
out of the peculiar forms and conftitutions
of them; but of thofe higher rights, which
belong to men as fuch, and which ought
to be preferved under all ftates and governments whatfoever. It is a branch of protection, which ought to be as effectually,
univerfally and impartially fecured, as pio-
tection in the enjoyment and exercife of any
other right, which can be named. — The extent of it again, or, to fpeak more precifely,
what is comprehended in the juft idea of it,

flows

flows from the fame principles with equal evidence. If liberty of confcience be a right effential to human nature, ALL penalties, in cafes merely of a religious nature, muft be an infringement of a right, and a DEGREE of OPPRESSION, though inflicted by a law: nor can the expreffion be juftly thought improper. Every law is oppreffive, which is unjuft; every law is unjuft, which fubverts the effential rights of mankind: and, if to judge for ourfelves in religion be one of the firft and moft inviolable of all thofe, which have ever been dignified with this title; it is evident, that every hardfhip, laid upon men for ufing it, is a degree of oppreffion, which the complete and perfect idea of Toleration excludes. And, from the fame principles, it can furely be no difficult matter to determine WHO are entitled to this protection. For this does not depend on the fuppofed truth or error of the fentiments which men may adopt; but upon the common right which all men have, to be led in thefe points by the light of their own minds, and to enjoy all the fecurities and benefits of fociety, while they fulfil the obligations of it. All, who can give good fecurity to the government, under which they live, and to the community to which they belong, for the performance of the duties of good fubjects and good citizens, have an undoubted claim to it, and cannot with any

juft

juſt reaſon be deprived of it. If, indeed,
there are any, whoſe religious principles put
it out of their power to give ſuch aſſurances
of this, as may be ſafely truſted, their caſe
may be thought an excepted one; though
in ſtrictneſs of ſpeech ſuch caſes are not ſo
properly exceptions from the rule laid down,
as caſes, which can never with reaſon be ſuppoſed to be included in it; for to ſay, that
all, who give proper, ſatisfactory pledges for
their being faithful ſubjects, have a right to
Toleration, can never give thoſe the ſame
right to it, who are incapable of giving ſuch
pledges. But whatever ſuch caſes may at
any time appear, or be ſuppoſed now to exiſt,
the principle upon which this argument is
conducted ſtands untouched. It is not on
account of their miſtakes in religion, but
their incapacity to be ſteady friends to the
ſtate, that they are laid under reſtraints. To
fix theſe reſtraints upon any other footing,
would be rendering them utterly indefenſible.
It is not error, but injury to the ſtate, or
the individuals, who are under the care of
it, which juſtifies the animadverſion of the
magiſtrate; and all, to whom this cannot be
juſtly imputed, are the objects of his protection: nor ought it to make any difference,
in this reſpect, what are the comparative
numbers of thoſe different bodies of men,
which compoſe the ſociety. As the magiſtrate

trate is not to attempt to diftrefs any of them, becaufe they differ from him in judgment; fo neither is he at liberty to facrifice one part to the clamour and bigotry of the other; but, as the common defender of juftice, equity and peace, impartially to preferve the freedom of them all. And here this part of the fubject might be dimiffed, were it not that the intervention of eftablifhments of religion makes, in the opinion of many, a great alteration in the extent of this religious liberty; for which reafon there feems to be a neceffity of confidering the grounds, and confequences of them a little diftinctly.

That eftablifhments cannot be juftly founded on a right in the magiftrate to impofe his own fentiments in religion upon his people, muft, if the reafonings hitherto purfued are allowed to be folid, be fufficiently clear. For whence can this right arife ? It cannot accrue to him by virtue of his office. That is merely civil; and for him to affume the direction of confcience in confequence of it would be going beyond the end of his power, and exceeding the bounds of his authority. It cannot be given him by the confent of his fubjects. — To give up the independence of confcience upon merely human authority, to any government, is making a facrifice to it, which they have no right to make. — In this fenfe, they are not at liberty to call any man mafter

ter upon earth; and from hence it is no obfcure, nor diftant, but a near and obvious inference, that to fuppofe the office of the magiftrate juftifies him in demanding fuch a fubmiffion from thofe, who are under his power, is to make it incompatible with religion, and fetting the duties of the man and the citizen at irreconcileable variance. — Let it be ferioufly confidered to what this leads. If religion has a real foundation, and the obligations of it are immutable, and yet no man can become a fubject of civil government, without implicitly refigning his confcience into the hands of the magiftrate; upon this fuppofition, I fay, (for, let it be obferved, it is only upon this fuppofition that this argument is formed) fubmiffion to magiftracy will be unjuftifiable, and government itfelf will be fhaken: fince it affumes to itfelf an authority, which no earthly power can claim, and exacts a fubjection which no man can have a right to yield. — If, again, to fupport government on this principle, it fhould be afferted, that the magiftrate has fuch an authority over confcience, what becomes of religion? For a proper authority in the governor to prefcribe, will always bring with it a correfpondent obligation, on the governed, to obey: nor is this confequence to be evaded by faying, that, in fuch cafes, a man muft be willing to fubmit to fuf-

E.   ferings,

ferings, rather than do evil. Where a rule of truth and duty is acknowledged independent on, and fuperior to, the pleafure of the magiftrate, this reply is good. But if the direction of the magiftrate is allowed to be the rule of our CONSCIENCE, or the ftandard, by which we are to govern our fentiments, and practice, in points relating to GOD; conformity to it will become the higheft principle of our actions, and whatever he enjoins muft of courfe be our duty. However he models, enlarges, or contracts religion, (let it be remembered this argument is ftill conducted upon this fuppofition only) it is our part to obey; and, though he fhould command things contrary even to his own confcience, which from political or other views is very poffible, we muft be bound in confcience to comply. And is this, I was going to afk, a principle which can be adopted by any one, who knows what religion and virtue mean, and is animated with a fincere regard to either? But it is needlefs. To afcribe fuch a power as this to any earthly fuperior is in reality to annihilate religion; and, inftead of fuppofing it to have a real immoveable foundation in truth, to refolve it all into the will of a fallible mortal. Nor will it be eafy for perfons to extricate themfelves from the difficulties, which thus prefs them clofe on both fides,

till

till they are brought to feparate the power
of the magiftrate to .guard the rights and
fafety of the fubject, and maintain his own
authority for that purpofe, from a right to
affume a jurifdiction over confcience, which
belongs to a much higher tribunal ; and thus,
while they render unto Cæfar the things
which are Cæfar's, referve for God, the
things which are God's.

The only juft, reafonable and honourable
conception of human eftablifhments of religion, is that of PROVISIONS made by the
governors of a ftate, for advancing the
knowledge and practice of religion and virtue.   According to this idea they ftand on
the fame bafis, and may properly be referred to the fame general rank, with all publick inftitutions for the cultivation of the
minds, and improvement of the morals of
men : only, when well conftructed, incom-
parably fuperior to them all, in weight, influence, and dignity.   They are in our own
country, if I may be allowed the expreffion, (in which I am fure not the moft
diftant thought of difrefpect to our ecclefiaftical eftablifhment is admitted) they are, I
fay, INCORPORATIONS by the legiflature for
the propagation of the gofpel at home ; and,
by a wife profecution of the ends of them,
may be productive of fingular benefits to the
prefent and future interefts of men.   But
E 2   then,

then, confidered in this light, I apprehend
they cannot be deemed LAWS for the whole
COMMUNITY, and univerfally binding on the
members of it; but endowments in favour of
thofe, who comply with the terms of them,
and fubmit to the regulations enjoined by
them. As human appointments they may
be examined, and have any defects attending
them calmly pointed out; and methods for
the improvement of them may be laudably
fuggefted. Whatever political neceflities may
in fome cafes have given rife to provifions to
the contrary, in themfelves they muft certainly be alterable : and as it is a principle, in all
well conftituted governments, that no particular inftitutions erected by them, fhould
contradict thofe primary maxims, by which
all civil focieties ought to be guided; fo it
muft be farther allowed, that eftablifhments of
religion themfelves fhould be regulated with
a religious regard to thefe maxims. Proceed-
ing now upon thefe data, it will be eafy to
arrive at the proper conclufion. For if, in
all human focieties, the religious rights of all
men ought to be preferved to them inviolable; if it be a maxim too certain to be denied, and too important to be given up, that
every man in the choice of his religion, is
to confider himfelf as accountable to God,
and bound to worfhip him according to HIS
will, and not according to the commandment
of

of men ; if thefe are truths, there can be no
difficulty in difcerning, that all forcible methods of bringing perfons to comply with
religious eftablifhments are abfolutely · unwarrantable. No encroachments on the native, original, rights of men, to procure
them a more extenfive reception, can be
juftified. Perfuafion alone is the inftrument,
by which they fhould gain ground. — The
evidence of their doctrines, the goodnefs of
their inftitutions, and their conformity to
the great ftandard, by which they are con-
feffedly to be tried, are the only arguments
by which they are to be recommended ;
and no power fhould be annexed to them,
or exerted in favour of them, to compel
fuch as diffent from them to embrace them.
Upon what principle, indeed, can the ufe
of fuch coercive meafures be juftified ? Of
themfelves, eftablifhments can claim no authority to employ force for this purpofe.
The civil power gives them their exiftence,
invefts them with their privileges, and con-
fers upon them every diftinction, which they
poffefs. If the magiftrate has no right to
exercife dominion over confcience, in himfelf,
he can impart no fuch right to them ; nor
can they acquire it in confequence of his
appointment : for, however he may think
proper to encourage the members of them,
the limits of his power, with refpect to the

other

other members of the community, are ftill the fame. Their common rights, as good 'fubjects, are not deftroyed or leffened; nor can any zeal for his own fentiments, or the fentiments of one part of his fubjects, vindicate his withholding his protection from the other. And no judicious friend of eftablifhments can be difpleafed with the manner in which thefe points are here ftated, or think it has any unfriendly afpect, on the ufefulnefs and honour of fuch appointments. Thofe, who are for building them on the ruins of the rights of human nature, and can never be fatisfied that they are fafe, or can be permanent, till all, who in any inftance depart from them, are brought into fubjection to them, are, in fact and eventually, their moft dangerous enemies. It is from this exceffive zeal for them, that fome of the ftrongeft prejudices againft thefe inftitutions have derived their exiftence. To reprefent them as carrying fuch claims with them is, in reality, taking the fureft way to difcredit them; and the greateft harveft of profelytes, gathered by fuch means, would be no acceffion to their praife, or any advantage to the caufe of religion. " Cultus dei nullus eft nifi ab animo vo- " lente procedat. — Voluntas autem docendo " & fuadendo elicitur : non MINIS non vi. " Coactus qui credit, non credit fed credere " fe fimulat ut malum vitet. Qui mali fen-
" fu

" fu aut metu extorquere affenfum vult, eo
" ipfo oftendit fe argumentis diffidere." Grot.
de Verit. R. C. Lib. vi. §. 7.

In all the views then, which have been
taken of this fubject, the refult is the fame;
that liberty in matters of religion is the
right of all; that a right to protection from
the magiftrate is the juft confequence of their
claim to this liberty; and that no difference
of opinion, refpecting modes of worfhip, or,
in a word, any thing, which does not inter-
fere with the rights of others, can juftify
his laying any reftraints upon it.   And great
would be the pleafure to every liberal mind,
if, amidft all the inftances of a wife and
vigorous attention to other branches of liberty, which run through the general fyftem
of our excellent laws, this alfo had been
kept more fteadily in view.   But to the
religious rights of men, it is apprehended
that feveral of our laws are not altoge-
ther fo favourable; and if, upon an application of the principles, here advanced on
the fubject of Toleration, to them, this fhall
be found to be the cafe, it is hoped that
pointing it out will give no offence.   To
fay of the beft code of human ftatutes that
they are not without defects, can be no un-
due prefumption; nor can defiring to have
thefe defects removed have any thing in it
inconfiftent with the character of the beft
                                                  friends

friends to our conftitution. And if in this part of my defign feveral particulars fhould be mentioned, which have been more than once laid before the publick ; it is not becaufe there is the leaft defire to give difguft to any perfons among us, or becaufe any pleafure is taken in the recital ; but for this reafon only, that if they were omitted, the juftice and weight of the reflections made upon the fubject could not be underftood.

Laws relating to Diffenters from the eftablifhed religion in popifh reigns have no concern here. They are all, it is prefumed, either formally or virtually repealed. But upon the revival of the reformation, an act was paffed, [h] by which it is enacted, that all, who " have " no lawful, or reafonable excufe to be abfent, " fhall endeavour themfelves to refort to " their parifh church, &c. where common " prayer fhall be ufed, upon pain of punifh- " ment by the cenfures of the church, and " upon pain that every perfon fo offending, " fhall forfeit, for every fuch offence, twelve " pence." By a fecond ftatute, [i] paffed in the fame reign, the fame offence, in every perfon above the age of fixteen years, fubjects the offender to a fine of twenty pounds for every month,

h Statutes at large, by Bafket and Lintot, 1758. vol. ii. i Eliz. cap. 2. §. 14.
i 23 Eliz. cap. 1. §. 5.

month, during which he shall so offend;
and if the said offence shall be continued
for a twelvemonth, he shall " over and
besides the said forfeitures," be bound with
two sufficient securities in the sum of two
hundred pounds at least, to his good behaviour, and this bond to continue in force
until they " conform themselves, and come
" to the church, according to the true mean-
" ing of the statute made in the first year of
" her Majesty's reign." In the 29th of the
same reign, another act was passed, to enforce
that just mentioned of the 23d; and after that
the celebrated act of the 35th of Eliz. took
place, by which, attendance on the service of
the common prayer is again required;[k] and
all persons above the age of sixteen, who, besides absenting themselves from the established
divine service for the space of a month, shall
be present at any assembly, conventicle, or
meeting, under pretence of any exercise of
religion, contrary to the laws and statutes of
the realm, are made subject to imprisonment,
in which they are to remain till they conform,
and make such submission and declaration of
conformity, as is afterwards enjoined.[l] ——
All offenders who do not, within three months
after conviction, conform and make such submission, upon warning by the act prescribed,
are obliged to abjure the realm; and it is

F

farther

---

[k] 35 Eliz. cap. i. §. 1, 2.   [l] Sect. 3. ejusd. cap.

farther enacted, that if they either refuse to abjure, or if, after abjuration made, they do not depart; or if, after their departure, they return without special licence from her Majesty, in every such case, the person offending shall be adjudged a felon, and suffer as in cases of felony, without benefit of clergy.

In the two following reigns little occurs in the statutes which is very material to my present purpose. Some acts indeed were passed, in the time of James I. against recusants, containing some clauses, which, it is implied in the act of Toleration, might, as well as those mentioned, be extended to protestant dissenters; but of these I shall not enter into any detail. From the 4th year of Charles I. to the 16th no English parliament was held; the first called that year was almost instantly dissolved, [m] and, after the meeting of the second, confusions broke out; a total subversion of the established church ensued; a new ecclesiastical polity rose up in its room; and ordinances in many respects equally severe, and repugnant to all the principles of charity, justice and humanity, with those which have been mentioned, were published by the powers, which had then the ascendant, in support of it. But soon after the Restoration things returned into their former channel,

[m] It met the 13th of April, and was dissolved the 5th of May. Macauley's Hist.

channel, and new laws againſt thoſe, who did not conform to the eccleſiaſtical eſtabliſhment were introduced; of which notice muſt be taken. The celebrated act of uniformity, 1662, forbids [n] any perſon, not having epiſcopal ordination, to celebrate the Lord's Supper, under the penalty of one hundred pounds for every offence; another clauſe of the ſame act declares, [o] that every perſon, who is by that act *diſabled,* [and the 15 Car. II. cap. vi. ſect. 7. adds *prohibited* from preaching,] who ſhall during ſuch diſability preach any ſermon or lecture, ſhall be impriſoned for three months. By ſect. 8. of the ſame act it is enacted that every ſchoolmaſter, though only teaching youth in any houſe, or private family, ſhall ſubſcribe a declaration containing, among other things, a promiſe to [p] conform to the liturgy of the church of England as by law eſtabliſhed; and it is added [q] that if any ſchoolmaſter, or other perſon teaching youth in any private houſe or family, ſhall undertake ſuch inſtruction before licence obtained, from the arch biſhop, biſhop, or ordinary of the dioceſe, and " before " ſuch ſubſcription and acknowledgment," as is by this act enjoined, he ſhall, for the firſt offence, ſuffer three months impriſonment, and for the ſecond, and every other offence,

F 2   ſuffer

---

[n] §. 14 of the act.   [o] §. 21.   [p] §. 9.
[q] §. 11.

fuffer the fame imprifonment, with the additional penalty of the forfeiture of five pounds.
Before this, by the very firft act ʳ of this fef-
fion, it had been made criminal for five or more
of the perfons called quakers, of or above the
age of fixteen, to affemble themfelves at one
time in any place, under pretence of joining
in a religious worfhip not authorized by the
laws of this realm : the penalty appointed is
any fum not exceeding five pounds for the firft
offence, or ten pounds for the fecond; and
for want of diftrefs, or in cafe of non-payment
within a week, imprifonment and hard labour
for the fpace of three months for the firft
offence, fix for the fecond : and for the third
offence it is enjoined, that they fhall either
abjure the realm, or be liable to tranfpor-
tation; unlefs they take fuch oath or oaths ˢ
for which they ftand committed, and give
fecurity that they will, for time to come,
forbear to meet in any fuch unlawful affembly : in which cafe they are difcharged of
the penalties aforefaid. In the year 1665,
the act for reftraining non-conformifts from
inhabiting in corporations, generally known
at that time, and mentioned by writers
fince, by the name of the five mile act, was
paffed. ᵗ By this ftatute, all parfons, &c.
who have not declared their unfeigned affent,
&c.

ʳ 13, 14 Car. II. cap. i. §. 2.   ˢ §. 5,
ᵗ 17 Car. II. cap. ii.

&c. and have not fubfcribed the declaration
contained in fect. 9. of the late act of uniformity, " and fhall not take the oath prefcribed
by this act, (and all perfons preaching in any
unlawful affembly,) are forbidden, till they
have taken this oath, to refide within five
miles of any town, which fends members to
parliament, or of any place, wherein they had,
fince the act of oblivion, been parfons, &c.
under the penalty of forty pounds for each
offence ; and, upon refufal of the oath, after
fuch offence fworn againft them, are liable to
imprifonment for fix months. And fuch perfons are farther enjoined," " to frequent divine
" fervice, as eftablifhed by the laws of this
" kingdom," or elfe to abftain from teaching
publick or private fchool, or from taking any
boarders or tablers, to be inftructed by themfelves or by any other, upon pain of forfeiting,
in like manner for every fuch offence, the fum
of forty pounds. And this was followed, in
the 22d year of the fame reign, by another
act againft conventicles, x which fubjects every perfon of the age of fixteen years, who
fhall be prefent at any affembly, &c. under
colour or pretence of any exercife of religion,
in other manner than according to the liturgy
and practice of the church of England, to a
fine of five fhillings for the firft offence, y and
of ten fhillings for every fucceeding one. z

The

---

u 13, 14 Car. II. cap. iv.   w §. 4.   x 22 Car. II.
cap. i.   y §. 1.   z §. 2.

The preacher at every fuch affembly is liable to the penalty of twenty pounds for the firft offence, and of forty pounds for each fucceeding one. [a] By the fame act, a fine of five pounds is impofed on all conftables, &c. who fhall willingly omit giving information, of fuch meetings or conventicles held within his precincts, &c. to fome juftice of the peace, or the chief magiftrate; [b] and then it is declared, [c] contrary to the general rule with refpect to all penal ftatutes, [d] viz. that they muft be conftrued ftrictly, that " this " act and all claufes therein contained, fhall " be conftrued moft largely and beneficially " for the fuppreffing of conventicles, and " for the juftification and encouragement of " all perfons to be employed in the execu- " tion thereof." Upon this footing I apprehend the laws againft affemblies for religious worfhip, in any manner not conformable to the eftablifhed, remained during the refidue of that reign, and through the reign which fuccceeded it. What alteration was made in them, by the act of Toleration, will be more properly confidered hereafter; in the mean time let us take a review of them, as far as this account has been continued.

And nothing, I think, can be more evident than that, through the whole tenor of
them

[a] §. 3.   [b] §. 11.   [c] §. 13.
[d] Blackftone's Comment. introd. §. 3. p. 83.

them, non-conformity, mere fimple non-conformity to the eftablifhed worfhip, and joining in religious worfhip in any manner not
according to the practice of the church of
England, are confidered as proper objects of
punifhment by the civil power, and loaded with
heavy penalties. I am fenfible it may be faid,
and juftice requires it fhould be acknowledged,
that feveral of thefe laws were originally or
chiefly levelled againft the roman catholicks, [e]
and that the incurable enmity which they dif-
covered to the perfon and government of
Queen Elizabeth, was the caufe of their being
paffed. It may poffibly be faid farther, that
as the roman catholicks were the perfons
againft whom the penalties of thefe acts
were chiefly intended, fo abfenting from
church is confidered in them as a mark of
popifh diffaffection, and that it is for this
reafon fuch a ftrong guard is placed againft
it. Let this alfo be admitted, as far as
it can with any juftice be defired. It muft
neverthelefs be acknowledged, that the bare
act of abfenting from the eftablifhed worfhip,
abftracted from any connexion with other obnoxious circumftances, is prohibited—that in
confequence of thefe laws, thofe penalties
might fall, indifcriminately, on all who did
not comply with thefe claufes of them ; and,

from

---

[e] Preamble to 13 Eliz. cap. ii. Heads of cap. i.
and preamble to 23 of Eliz. cap. i.

from 1662 to the Revolution, it will not be
difputed, I imagine, but the whole body
of thofe, who did not join in the eftablifhed
worfhip, were fuppofed to be comprehended
under them. [f] The act of the 1ft of Elizabeth, appears to be directly and originally
intended againft ALL who did not thus conform. The act of the 35th of Elizabeth
muft be allowed to be aimed againft fectaries
in general: and, whoever is acquainted with
the ftate of things at the paffing of it, will
have little doubt but that it was defigned to
affect the puritans, if not principally, yet
equally with any other. If I had faid it was
contrived almoft folely with a view to them, I
fhould not, I prefume, have erred; fince it is
declared in the fame act, [g] that no popifh
recufant fhall be compelled or bound to
abjure, by virtue of it. That it was on
account of PROTESTANT diffenters from the
national form of worfhip, that all the laws
made in the time of Charles II. which I have
been now enumerating, that it was, I fay, on
their account, that thefe ftatutes were paffed,
and againft them that they were immediately
intended to operate, is univerfally allowed.
ROMAN CATHOLICKS, it is well known, were
the

[f] The ftatute of 16 Car. II. cap. iv. for fuppreffing
of feditious conventicles exprefly declares the 35th of
Eliz. to be in force, and that it ought to be put in
execution.

[g] §. 12.

the FAVOURED party, with fome of thofe at
the helm, during a confiderable part of that
reign. Whatever was done to reftrain them
was extorted by the voice and the murmurs
of the people, and the remonftrances of the
two houfes, when they began to be aware of
the defigns of the court. The proteftant non-
conformifts were the obnoxious fet of men,
who were to be harraffed and oppreffed.
No fhort indulgencies were granted them,
but what were fufpected, at leaft, to proceed
from fome dangerous defigns; and when it
was found that no ftratagem was effectual to
bring them to countenance meafures, which
they judged inconfiftent with the liberties of
their country, and hazardous to the intereft
of the proteftant religion, all the power,
which the laws had thrown into the hands
of their enemies, was exerted to crufh them
with as much eagernefs as ever.

Now, in order to juftify thefe laws, it
muft be fuppofed that non-conformity is in
ITSELF a crime, and a very heinous one.
For to fay that the laws have made it a
crime is faying nothing: fince, upon this
principle, there is no action, how innocent,
how laudable foever, but what may be con-
verted into a crime, and the law, by which it
is punifhed, may be vindicated. If this method of reafoning be juft, it was a crime in
Daniel to perfift in his devotions after they

G   were

were forbidden by the decree of Darius; and the death, which the enemies of that noble example of fortitude in the worſhip of the true God, inſiſted on his ſuffering, was no more than he merited. By this argument it was criminal in any of the Jews to acknowledge Jeſus as the Meſſiah, becauſe it had been made a rule among them, that if any man did confeſs that Jeſus was the Chriſt, he ſhould be put out of the ſynagogue. When the ſpirit and fitneſs of any laws are under conſideration, the determining point is, what reaſons there were, antecedently to their being enacted, to induce the legiſlators to adopt them; and the queſtion in all PENAL laws in particular muſt be, whether the thing prohibited by them is in itſelf a juſt object of puniſhment. If this great requiſite to their juſtification be wanting, all attempts to defend them will be impotent and vain.

To aſſert, that non-conformity to the eſtabliſhed religion of any country, is in itſelf an offence againſt the ſtate, is to maintain a poſition unſupported by ſcripture, reaſon and experience, and indeed confuted by every one of them. St. Paul evidently ſuppoſes, that non-conformiſts might be the beſt of ſubjects to the civil magiſtrate, when he enjoins chriſtians, whoſe religious principles ſtood in the moſt direct oppoſition to the eſtabliſhed worſhip of the heathens, to be " ſubject to the
" higher

" higher powers,"[h] and commands that they
fhould be taught to be " fubject to principa-
" lities and powers, to obey magiftrates, and
" to be ready to every good work."[i] St. Peter
muft have been fully convinced that difapprobation of the authorized religion of the
Roman empire was perfectly confiftent with
loyalty to the rulers of it, when he requires
thofe to whom he wrote,[k] " to be fubject to
" every ordinance of man for the Lord's
" fake; whether to the emperor[l] as fupreme,
" or unto governors as unto thofe, who are
" fent by him for the punifhment of evil-
" doers, and the praife of them that do well : "
and yet, while he warns none of them to
fuffer as evil-doers, encourages them, if they
fuffer as chriftians, not to be afhamed, but
to glorify God on this account. Where indeed is the repugnance between not affenting
to the eftablifhed worfhip, and retaining at
the fame time the warmeft affection to the
welfare of the ftate ? Men may yield fubjection to the civil laws of their country, and
bear their fhare of the publick burthens ; be
zealoufly attached to their fovereign, benevo-
lent to their fellow fubjects, unite with them
in their endeavours to fupport the authority of
the government, and to refift their common
enemies whether foreign or domeftick ; and,

G 2   in

<hr>

[h] Romans xiii. 1.   [i] Titus iii. 1.
[k] 1 Ep. ii. 13.   [l] Grot. & Beza on the verfe.

in a word, enter chearfully into every meafure, which is neceffary to advance the peace,
profperity, and reputation of the community,
though they may differ widely in their religious fentiments from their fuperiors, or from
the majority of thofe about them. Nor is
this mere theory. — It is certain and notori-
ous fact. In Switzerland we have an inftance
which comes nearly up to this. There proteftant and popifh cantons are all vigorous
in keeping a confederacy, for the prefervation of their common liberty, unbroken. In
the United Provinces we have an inftance
which comes nearer to it ftill. Calvinifts, arminians, and other religious denominations of
that republick, have unanimoufly fhown themfelves ready to affert its freedom; purfued
the intereft of their country with unremitting
attention; and, notwithftanding all their variety of religious tenets, live amicably one
with another. Our own nation has for many
years happily afforded us a cafe of this nature, which is fully in point; and whoever
looks back to the year 1745, and recollects
the fervour and animated refolution, with
which all parties among us rofe up, as one
man, to repel the attempt, which was then
made, to fubvert the fettlement of the illuftrious houfe of Hanover in the throne of
thefe kingdoms, and defend the wife and be-
neficent conftitution, from which they derive
                                        fuch

fuch invaluable bleffings : whoever attends
to this, and to the friendly intercourfe, which
fubfifts between the members of our religious eftablifhment, and thofe, who in fome
refpects differ from it, will want no farther
confirmation of what is here afferted. It is indeed only a contracted view of things, which
can lead any to call it in queftion. And if any
inftances fhould be fuppofed to occur in hiftory to the contrary, it will be found, upon
examination, that they have never been really
occafioned by the juft principles of religious
liberty. The non-tolerating fpirit has been
the true fource of them ;

" Hoc fonte derivata clades
" In patriam, populumque fluxit."

If non-conformity then is in itfelf no offence againft the ftate, and yet diffenters, as
fuch, are ftill confidered as the proper fubject of punifhment, from what principles
muft this judgment be formed of them ?
From thefe, and thefe only, that all perfons
are bound to take their fentiments in religion
from the legiflature : — that it is a duty incumbent on them, to acquiefce in, and conform to, what the ruling powers eftablifh ; and
that to feparate from it, and conduct religious worfhip in a manner not prefcribed by
them, is a fufficient reafon for inflicting penalties

nalties upon thofe, who are convicted of it. From thefe maxims the laws, which are now under confideration, derive their exiftence; and whoever carefully weighs the language, and enters into the fpirit of them, will find that thefe are the principles which are implied in every one of them. It is true, indeed, that different reafons are affigned in the laws themfelves for paffing them. The 35th of Elizabeth, fo often mentioned, is faid to be "for the preventing and avoiding "of fuch great inconveniencies and perils, " as might happen and grow by the wicked " and dangerous practices of feditious fecta- " ries and difloyal perfons." [m] But, befides what has been fuggefted of thefe acts in general, and is particularly true of this, that they are fo conftructed as to involve all, whether peaceable or feditious, loyal or difloyal non-conformifts, in one common condemnation; it will perhaps be found that mere diffenting from, and cenfuring fome appointments of, the eftablifhed religion, are the very grounds, in part at leaft, upon which this fedition is laid to their charge. And this appears to me evident from the fubmiffion, which, by this act, perfons who had tranfgreffed it were allowed and required to make, in order to avoid the penalties which they had incurred; and which, as it may poffibly never have been feen,

---

[m] See the beginning of the act.

feen, or perhaps fo much as heard of, by
fome perfons, into whofe hands this effay may
fall, is here tranfcribed.' " (1) I A. B. do
" humbly confefs and acknowledge, that I
" have grievoufly offended God in contemn-
" ing her Majefty's godly and lawful go-
" vernment and authority, by abfenting my-
" felf from church, and from hearing divine
" fervice, contrary to the godly laws and
" ftatutes of this realm, and in ufing and
" frequenting difordered and unlawful con-
" venticles and affemblies, under pretence
" and colour of exercife of religion ; (2)
" and I am heartily forry for the fame,
" and do acknowledge and teftify in my
" confcience, that no other perfon hath,
" or ought to have, any power or autho-
" rity over her Majefty ; (3) and I do pro-
" mife and proteft, without any diffimula-
" tion, or any colour or means of any dif-
" penfation, that from henceforth I will, from
" time to time, obey and perform her Ma-
" jefty's laws and ftatutes in repairing to the
" church and hearing divine fervice, and do
" my uttermoft endeavour to maintain and
" defend the fame." ⁿ   And if from hence we
defcend to the laws of later date, which have
now been before us, we fhall find the fame,
or .fimilar principles interwoven with them,
and infeparable from them.   Thay clearly
fuppofe,

suppofe, that the rule enjoined by the government is the rule, to which every perfon in the realm is to conform in publick worfhip.——That his non-compliance with it brings him under a guilt cognizable by human tribunals, and juftifies the magiftrate in laying any penalties upon the fuppofed delinquents, which fhall be judged neceffary to compel them to fubmiffion. To go on to enquire, after this, how far fuch laws are reconcileable to the principles of Toleration, would be almoft an affront to the underftanding of the reader. More has been faid already than would have been thought needful, were it not for the implicit approbation, which fome may give to thefe laws without ever reflecting on the foundation of them.——On this account it was thought requifite to trace them up to their firft principles ; and nothing can be clearer, than that they ftand in the fulleft oppofition to all claims of religious liberty. According to thefe, in matters relating to God, every man is to judge for himfelf. But thefe laws virtually affert, that the magiftrate has a right to judge for him. The principles of Toleration affirm, that, for the ufe of this merely religious liberty, no man ought to be hurt with refpect to his peace, freedom or eftate. Thefe laws imply, that for this caufe alone, he may be punifhed with refpect to all thefe interefts :

that

that is, in other words, that he may be
perfecuted for confcience fake; for thefe are
the very principles upon which perfecution
relies for its defence: they are pregnant with
all the evils of which that dreadful iniquity is
productive; and, wherever they are admitted,
vindicated, and the effects of them juftified,
the principles of Toleration are fo far excluded. To be confiftent advocates for the continuance of penalties founded on fuch a bafis,
and friends to the rights of confcience in
their due extent, is impoffible. So long as
thefe laws remained in their full force and
extent; fo long as they were the rule of
judgment upon all thofe who thought themfelves bound to diffent from the ecclefiaftical
eftablifhment; no liberty of choofing any
kind of religious publick worfhip but that,
which was commanded by the government
was acknowledged to belong to the fubjects
of it. All fuppofition of any right in perfons to be tolerated in departing from points
determined by that eftablifhment, was fo far
from being fuffered to take place, that it
was rejected as utterly inadmiffible, and a
power virtually afcribed to the magiftrate of
prefcribing, to thofe under his jurifdiction,
whatever articles and forms of religion he might
think proper. For the fame principles, by
which conformity to thefe doctrines, and modes
of worfhip was required, might, with equal

juſtice, have been applied to any others enjoined in like manner; the ſame arguments
which were urged for inflicting puniſhments
on thoſe who refuſed ſubmiſſion in caſes
already ſettled, would have been judged
equally clear and cogent for the uſe of them
in all others of a ſimilar nature; and no
pleas of conſcience, how ſincere ſoever, would
have been allowed as a ſufficient reaſon for
exemption from them.

When the ever-memorable and auſpicious
Revolution had taken place, the ſeverity of
theſe laws was exchanged for a toleration of
the ſentiments and worſhip of thoſe perſons,
who had ſo long and greatly ſuffered in conſe-
quence of them; and the dawn of conſtitu-
tional religious liberty broke in upon the
kingdom. The diſſenters joyfully and gratefully owned the alteration, which was made
in their favour; and it is with the ſame diſpoſitions, that the diſſenters of theſe days
look back to the relief, which was then
granted to their predeceſſors, and attend to
the happy conſequences, which may be conſidered as reſulting from it to themſelves. It
is with a degree of pain that they find themſelves under a neceſſity of ſpeaking of it as
in any meaſure inadequate to the relief of
thoſe, who, upon the right principles of Toleration, ought to be placed in ſecurity. But
if the limitations contained in it be conſidered.

dered, it will appear that the eafe given by it to confcientious diffenters, though great, was not abfolutely a complete one, even at the time of its paffing. In thefe days it is much lefs fo. The great changes which the religious fentiments of all denominations in the kingdom have undergone fince, exclude great numbers who are entitled, upon all the principles of reafon and humanity, to enjoy religious liberty, from the benefits of it; and render the Toleration which is granted by it, in fact, a very defective, contracted one; and that not only in the light of political juftice, but I believe it may be added, upon the very principles of many of the moft eminent adverfaries to any extenfion of it.

The quakers, it is well known, are entitled to the advantages of the act of Toleration,° upon fubfcribing the declaration againft tranfubftantiation, making a declaration of fidelity to the government, profeffing their belief in the Father, Son, and Holy Ghoft, as one God, and acknowledging the infpiration of the Holy Scriptures. But, in order to be comprehended in thefe claufes, it muft furely be neceffary for a man to profefs himfelf a quaker; and every preacher among the diffenters, who cannot do this, muft either fubfcribe to all the other articles of the church, excepting the 34th, 35th, 36th, part of the

H 2   20th,

° §. 13. compared with §. 2.

20th, and that part of the 27th which relates
to infant baptifm, or be liable to all the
penalties to which he would have been fubject, had the act of Toleration never taken
place. Let it be confidered then who are,
by the tenor of this act, deprived of all advantages from it. —— By the 1ft and 2d articles, not only thofe, who openly contradict
the doctrine of the Trinity, as ftated in the
articles, but every one, who, from the difficulties which he may find attending it, is not
able to declare his affent to it, is debarred
from all the benefits of Toleration.—The 5th
article excludes all thofe, who think with the
Greek church concerning the proceffion of
the Holy Ghoft—And the 8th article, by declaring the creed of Athanafius to be one of
thofe which ought thoroughly to be received
and believed, will be thought by many to exclude all thofe, who DO BELIEVE this part of
the eftablifhed doctrine, if they cannot at the
fame time declare all thofe, who do not receive it, fubject, without doubt, to perifh
everlaftingly. — By the 17th, all thofe who
are diffatisfied with the doctrine of predefti-
nation, in what is commonly ftiled the calvi-
niftick fenfe of the doctrine, and, who are
neverthelefs perfuaded that in this fenfe it is
taught in the article, and that the profeffion
of it, in this fenfe, is implied in their fubfcription ; all thefe, I fay, are debarred from
the

the benefit of the act in like manner. To fay, they miftake the meaning of the article, does not leffen but, in the event, rather aggravates the hardfhip: fince, in this cafe, they are excluded, not for any error in doctrine, but merely by underftanding the article to teach a doctrine, which not only the language of it ftrongly favours; but which it was generally fuppofed to teach for many years after it received the fanction of authority; and which the commons in parliament, in the year 1628 [p] avowed, in OPPOSITION to the fenfe of the arminians, to be delivered by publick act of the church of England, and by the general and concurrent expofition of the writers of that church. It was, indeed, if bifhop Hoadley's authority may determine this matter, one of thofe points, which were once thought as fundamental and effential to orthodoxy, by numbers in the church of England, as they ftill are among fome proteftants, till, as he tells us, [q] archbifhop Laud altered the whole current of the received doctrine, and accommodated this doctrine fo altered, to the words of the articles firft framed upon another fcheme. — It will, again, be a matter of very ferious doubt, at leaft, with many, whether, in con-
                                        fequence

[p] Macauley's hift. vol. ii. p. 35. 8vo. ed.

[q] Anfwer to the reprefentation of the committee, p. 268.

sequence of the subscription required to the 18th article among the rest, such as cannot bring themselves to deny salvation to the most virtuous heathens, and in a word to all those who have not heard of the gospel, are not excluded also. — And it is presumed it is out of all question, that all persons, who do not acknowledge, that the " fault or corruption of the nature of every " man, that naturally is engendered of the " offspring of Adam —— in every person " born into the world, deserveth God's wrath " and damnation; " [r] all, who ascribe to man, since the fall of Adam, an ability " to " turn and prepare himself by his own na- " tural strength and good works, to faith and " calling upon God; " [s] and all those, who scruple to affirm, that " works done before " the grace of Christ and the inspiration of " his Spirit, are not pleasant to God; " [t] and know not how to say they " doubt not that " they [such works] have rather the nature " of sin : " there is no question, it is apprehended, but that all, who are included in this number, will, if subscription implies belief, be incapable of deriving any security from this act. —— Let these particulars now be weighed, and how narrow will the limits of this Toleration appear ? Were the establishment of the church of England now to

be

[r] See article 9th.   [s] Article 10th.   [t] Article 13th.

be formed, or were it thought expedient to model the articles of it anew; the appeal is chearfully made to the laity, the clergy, and even to thofe, to whom the government of the church and clergy is committed, whether fubfcription to all thefe decifions would ftill be required ? Would they think it confiftent with the wifdom and charity, with which they would undoubtedly conduct fuch an undertaking, to make affenting to propofitions fo doubtful, and which have been the fubject of fo much controverfy, as fome of thefe are known to have been, the condition of being admitted to the miniftry ? Would they fix upon that as the center of union, which, inftead of uniting, muft divide; give uneafinefs to numbers of candid, thoughtful, and ingenuous minds; and perhaps keep many of thofe, whofe concurrence would be a ftrength and ornament to their caufe, from continuing among them ? As the eftablifhment is now conftituted, it is a fact univerfally known, that there are the wideft differences of fentiment, among the clergy of it, upon feveral of thefe topicks. So far is this from being accounted a reproach, that it is appealed to as a token of the extenfive charity and moderation of the church of England, that fuch freedom of thought fubfifts among thofe, who are received into her bofom. And, if they think it would be

wrong

wrong to infift upon greater uniformity of judgment in thofe of their own body, can it be reafonable to exact it from others, in order to their enjoyment of a Toleration ?. It is undoubtedly an error (and deferves to be efteemed a very great one) when doctrines of doubtful difputation, and uneffential to the intereft of religion, are bound upon the minifters of any church, and thofe, who cannot affent to them, are rejected as unfit to partake of the advantages, or difcharge the duties of that important character. The nearer any eftablifhments approach to pure, original chriftianity, and the more the genuine fpirit of the gofpel appears in them, with all its native luftre and fimplicity ; the more excellent, the more amiable they are in the eyes of their friends. The more fuperior to all the objections of their enemies they will always be found : and, wherever any advances are made in bringing any of them to greater degrees of this perfection, there is not a judicious advocate for truth and charity, who will not be ready to fay, with an illuftrious promoter of both ; *Bleffed be they who have contributed to fo good a work.* ᵘ But to contend for making doctrines greatly controverted, and which, if they were not already in poffeffion of a place among the articles of
the

ᵘ Bifhop Hoadley's poftfcript to his anfwer to Dr. Hare, p. 207.

the church, would perhaps never be admitted into the number: to contend, I ſay, for making theſe the boundaries of a Toleration, and, (which is the plain meaning of it, how harſhly ſoever the expoſition may ſound,) plead for leaving thoſe, who ſcruple aſſenting to them, ſubject to the terrors of fines, impriſonments, and all the hardſhips which theſe penalties may bring with them, hurts humanity itſelf. Theſe are ſeverities, which it ought not to be ſuppoſed one, even of thoſe gentlemen, who oppoſe making the act of Toleration more extenſive, would wiſh to take place. And I am perſuaded that I do no more than juſtice to the equity and candor of their diſpoſitions, when I ſay, that were the execution of the laws which ſtill ſtand in force, againſt all thoſe, who cannot come up to the conditions required by the act of Toleration, to be revived, they would find all the generous feelings of their hearts revolt at the conſequences. But what part then might it be expected every one, who profeſſes himſelf a friend to Toleration, when the queſtion comes before him, and waits for his ſober, impartial deciſion, ſhould chooſe? What? But to join in placing it on a more enlarged baſis, and procuring for thoſe, who requeſt it, that extenſive legal ſecurity, which the ſpirit of the goſpel requires they ſhould enjoy, and to which natural juſtice gives them an unqueſtionable title ?

And this, of courſe, brings on the conſideration of the ſtep, which the diſſenters ſo lately took, of applying for an enlargement of the liberties which are granted them by the act of Toleration. It may indeed be ſuppoſed that, if what has been ſaid be granted, all occaſion to add any thing farther upon the ſubject is precluded. And were the principles of religious liberty admitted in their juſt conſequences, and the nature of the application made by the diſſenters univerſally underſtood, it would be ſo. But ſince the attempt itſelf has been much miſapprehended ; ſince there are perſons, truly reſpectable for their underſtanding and character, who have ſo amazingly overlooked the natural inferences from their own principles, as to profeſs to adopt the moſt generous notions of Toleration, and yet ſhown themſelves utterly averſe from granting the relief requeſted ; it cannot be ſuperfluous to debate the queſtion. The reflections which the attempt has drawn upon the diſſenters, render it every way expedient ; and, far from deſerving to be thought an inſtance of over-officious zeal, it is but a mere act of juſtice to remove the objections which have been made to their conduct. The TIME and MANNER of their application are only circum-

ſtances.

ftauces, in which the merits of their cafe have little or no concern. It is the NATURE of their requeft, which is to détermine the judgment of every man relating to it : and if it fhall appear, that what they afked was reafonable in itfelf ; — that it was not afked without occafion ; — that the evils apprehended from granting it were either imaginary, or infufficient reafons for rejecting it ; — that their general character and conduct afford no ground to judge them unworthy of the liberty which they folicited ; — and that the terms upon which they defired to enjoy it, were adequate to every demand, which could reafonably be made upon them : — if thefe things fhall be found evident, it is prefumed their application ftands clear of exception, and will be found to aim at nothing contradictory to the principles of good fubjects, confiftent proteftants, and fincere chriftians.

Let the NATURE of their requeft be firft confidered. For if this was wrong in itfelf, the point is already decided. But upon what principle can this be afferted ? Will it be maintained that the laws from which they defire a farther exemption are, in themfelves, right and equitable ? If there be any remaining who can ferioufly retain this opinion, and think it fit that mere diffenters from the doctrines of the church fhould continue liable to legal penalties, it is natural for THEM

to

to efteem the matter of the requeft wrong,
In their apprehenfion the act of Toleration,
limited as it is, . muft be unreafonable;
and they muft judge, in oppofition to the
fenfe of our rulers, who firft paffed the act,
and the repeated and moft publick declarations of all the conftituent parts of the legiflature, that, inftead of being extended, it
ought not to be in any degree maintained, but
revoked, and that all the feverities of former
days fhould be acted over again. But it is
not to perfons of this complexion that the diffenters can be fuppofed to refer the merits of
their late petition. They founded their hopes
of fuccefs in a perfuafion, that perfecuting laws
were now allowed to be indefenfible; and that
the juftice of Toleration, and the political wifdom of it too, had the univerfal fuffrage. That
the matter of their petition therefore, fhould
be condemned, as wrong in itfelf, by gentlemen profeffing to efpoufe thefe fentiments, appears to them beyond explication. Whether
any of the articles, which the diffenters may
fcruple to fubfcribe, in any refpect vary
from the truth or not, is a point, into
which it is utterly needlefs here to enquire.
The queftion to be attended to is this; does
their doubt of any of them affect their character as good fubjects? Is their declining
to profefs their belief of a number of doctrinal propofitions, (the fenfe, of fome of which,
is difputed, and the certain meaning of others

of

of· them utterly contradicted, by numbers of
the ableft, moft learned, and moft refpectable.
of thofe, who enjoy the emoluments, which
are annexed to the eftablifhed church,) a fufficient ground to judge them unworthy of the
protection of the government ?· If not, it
muft ftill be a wonder, that any of the advocates for Toleration fhould affign the mere
matter of the requeft of the diffenters as a
caufe for rejecting it ; and will continue to be
fo till a very convincing reafon is affigned for
the refufal.   For it is to be confidered, that,
if Toleration be the general right of all, who
approve themfelves good members of fociety,
thofe, who OPPOSE it are the perfons, upon
whom it is incumbent to prove that it ought
not to be granted.

The author of the letter to the diffenting
minifters, who applied to parliament for relief, has, it muft be owned, attempted to
fhow this.   His reafon in fhort is, that the
act paffed for the relief of diffenters at the
Revolution, confines Toleration to matters of
difcipline only ; and that the Toleration then
granted to proteftant diffenters, as fuch,
could not be meant to extend farther than
to the points, in which they differed from
the national church, with which, at that time,
they agreed in points of doctrine. " Had
this reafoning been advanced by a perfon of
                                          lower

" See the letter, p. 4—11.

lower abilities, many would be difpofed to think that the bare ftating of this objection to the application of the diffenters, is, in effect, anfwering it, and that it might be fafely difmiffed without any reflections. But the deference due to a writer, who certainly difcovers much, both of the language and addrefs of a gentleman, in his manner of writing, requires that more particular notice fhould be taken of it. With fubmiffion to his authority then, it may be obferved, that his reprefentation of the act of Toleration itfelf is not perfectly exact. He fays, that the act " did not mean to tolerate doctrines " different from thofe of the chriftian church " in general." [x] How then came the body of the quakers to be included in it? Their doctrines, at that time, were certainly different, in fome refpects, from thofe that were generally held by the chriftian church ; and their denying the obligation of the facraments in particular, was a departure from the moft univerfal confent of the fentiments and practice of the chriftian church, which can be urged in favour of any points, which were ever called into queftion. Whoever attentively confiders the conftruction of the act of Toleration, and the judicious remarks, which the author of the cafe of the diffenters has made upon it, will find reafon to believe, that

[x] Letter, p. 9.

that the intention of the act was to com-
prehend all proteftants, who affented to the
received doctrine of the Trinity; and that
the meafure of their fubfcriptions, or declarations, relating to religious doctrines in other
particulars, was adjufted to the degree, in
which the feveral denominations of them
were known to approach to, or depart from,
the articles of the national church. Had not
this been their defign, it is inconceivable that
the quakers, who ftood at fo great a diftance from the eftablifhed church, in points
of doctrine as well as difcipline, fhould have
been comprehended in it, and " enjoy," as
the act exprefsly fays they fhall, " all the
" other benefits, privileges, and advantages,
" under the like limitations, &c. which any
" other diffenters fhall or ought to enjoy,
" by virtue of this act." ᵞ   And can it be
fuppofed then, that, if the prefbyterians or
independents had differed farther in their fentiments, than at that time they did, from the
articles of the church, the fame parliament,
which confulted in this manner the eafe of
that body, (which, ufeful and refpectable as
it is, was certainly the leaft popular, in refpect to religious fentiments, of all the other
tolerated bodies of men,) can it be fuppofed,
I fay, that, in this cafe, the eafe of the
other diffenters would not have been equally
con-

ᵞ §. 13.

confulted ?[z] But, admit the fact to be as this author has ftated it ; of what weight is it ? Is it a confequence, that becaufe that parliament went only thus far, fucceeding ones muft go no farther ? If the diffenters of thofe times needed nothing more to make them eafy, and therefore afked for nothing more, does that make it unreafonable for their fucceffors to afk and obtain more ? In a word, the queftion is not, what was formerly determined, but what the rights of confcience make it equitable for men to requeft, and for the legiflature to grant : and if the laws againft diffenters were wrong in themfelves, and thofe, who ftill lye open to them, have an equally juft plea to be placed out of the reach of their oppreffion with thofe, who are now fheltered from it ; nothing can be plainer than that they ought to be put in the fame fecure fituation ; and that the requeft of the diffenters was juft and good.

To fuppofe that Toleration is to be limited, by the articles of the national church, is, in effect, reducing the Toleration of proteftant diffenters to very little in this ; and, in all roman catholick countries, it is giving up the Toleration of the whole body of proteftants entirely. They differ from the national churches of the ftates, of which they are parts,

not

not only in difcipline, but in doctrines. Their
opinions are inconfiftent with thofe, which are
eftablifhed by law, in points, which the catholicks efteem fundamental;—in thofe which
concern the rule of faith, and the objects
of worfhip: and they have given it as their
judgment, that the honours paid to faints,
to images, and to the hoft, are nothing lefs
than idolatry. Will this writer therefore fay,
they ought not to be tolerated, but lie open
to the punifhment of the gallies, imprifon-
ments, and all the tortures of the inquifition? If he efteems this too abfurd to be
admitted, with what confiftency can he fuppofe, that the diffent of proteftants from
a PROTESTANT church, in fome points of
doctrine, deftroys their title to a legal Toleration? It is no juftification of this oppreffion, to dignify the principles, thus enforced
by penalties, with the founding titles of doctrines, which have been acknowledged by the
chriftian church in general, and the fuppofed
fundamentals of chriftianity. The confent
of all the churches upoo earth, in favour
of a doctrine, creates no obligation upon
others to receive it, in oppofition to their
convictions, that it is unfupported by fcripture; nor authorizes the application of penalties to enforce it. Chriftianity itfelf is not
to be propagated by the terrors and cruel-
ties of perfecution. It is not many ages

K   fince

fince tranfubftantiation, and all the mercilefs load of the other enormous corruptions and fuperftitions of popery, were " maintained " by all the eftablifhed churches of the weftern world, and it was efteemed impiety to dif- pute them. To infinuate, therefore, that perfons become unfit for a Toleration, by departing from thofe doctrines which an eftablifhed church, or all eftablifhed churches (if that expreffion is liked better) judge to be fundamental; to infinuate this, I fay, is fixing a brand upon the Reformation. It opens a door to oppreffion wherever fuch diffent from the publick religion is to be found, and, in a PROTESTANT, is fomething *aftonifhing.* Every church, as Mr. Locke obferves, and as it has been innumerable times obferved after him, is orthodox to herfelf, and judges her doctrines to be thofe of chriftianity. The church of Rome main- tains feveral of thofe doctrines, which are utterly REJECTED by proteftants, to be the ancient catholick faith of chriftianity; and, whatever fome of her more moderate mem- bers may do, in her publick, authentick acts, excludes all, who deny them, from being truly parts of the chriftian church. So that wherever the faith of THAT church is eftablifhed, all thofe who adhere to the doctrines of the REFORMATION, muft, upon this author's own principles, lofe their claim

to

to a Toleration. But there is a peculiar unreasonablenefs in confining this privilege within thefe limits, if, as he affirms, [a] there are doctrines inferted in the articles of the church, which were not intended by the compilers as credenda, or things neceffary to be believed. To be obliged to fubfcribe thefe is furely more than can be neceffary to a Toleration, even upon his own principles: nor is it any alleviation of the burthen, that the diffenting minifters were formerly fuppofed to approve them, and have actually affented to them in their writings. [b] Whether they approve them or not, the diffenting minifters are laid under the fame neceffity of fubfcribing THESE articles, as they are under to fubfcribe the moft fundamental doctrines, which can be named among the whole collection: and it very little mitigates the hardfhip, that they are fpoken of under the foftening title of articles of peace. [c] This is a diftinction in the articles, which the diffenters know not that they have any warrant from publick authority to make; and, if by this is meant, that they are only articles not to be oppofed, the anfwer is, that to declare an approbation of, and fubfcribe to an article, is, in the judgment of the diffenters in general, an act of

K 2   a very

---

[a] Letter, p. 7.   [b] Ibid. p. 7.   [c] Ibid. p. 9.

a very different amount from a bare promise to keep silence in relation to it.

But suppofing all this to be admitted in favour of the diffenters, their application is blamed by mauy, as being a needlefs one. The ftate of their cafe, delivered to the members of the two houfes, is fpoken of as dwelling upon appearances of a perfecution [d] which no where exifts, and only flipping as it were by accident, into an indirect acknow-ledgment that the violation of the law has been connived at. But was it poffible for the cafe to be otherwife drawn up? Does not every petition for the redrefs of grievances, carry in it a reprefentation of thofe grievances? Were the diffenters to lay before the legiflature their defires to be relieved from burthens, without fpecifying what thefe burthens were? To charge them, though ever fo indirectly, with an intention to infinuate, that they fuffer hardfhips from which they are entirely free, is to load them with an imputation of unfairnefs, for which they have given no caufe. Their complaint was not of the fpirit of the times, but of the fpirit of the laws, from which they hoped to be relieved. This, whether thofe laws are executed, or unexecuted, is in itfelf ftill the fame; and if the recital of the fubftance of them excites " horror and compaffion," [e] the

reproach

[d] Letter, p. 3.   [e] Ibid. ubi fup.

reproach falls upon them, and not upon the adminiftration of the government, the mild and gentle tenor of which is thankfully perceived, and chearfully owned, by every diffenter in the kingdom. But connivance is not legal Toleration ; non-execution of the penal laws, againft non-conformifts, is a very different thing from proper exemption from them. And, if this be what they are perfuaded they may reafonably afk, upon what principle they can be blamed, merely for making an application for it, is little fhort of being utterly incomprehenfible. Was it ever imputed to men as a crime, as an inftance of reftleffnefs, or even a want of decorum, that they defired not to be left open to oppreffion ? Or can it be any reafon for cenfuring perfons as not eafily fatisfied, ' that they are folicitous to be guarded from dangers, to which they are always expofed, and from which, though they have no immediate profpect of it, great evils may poffibly come upon them ? To fay, that the diffenters labour under no grievance, though in one fenfe it may be allowed, falls far fhort of the point. If the laws in queftion are in themfelves unreafonable ; if feveral of them were at firft dictated by a fpirit of revenge ; calculated for bad purpofes ; and may be made the inftruments of breaking in upon the

' Letter, p. 17.

the peace, property and liberty, of perfons
of the moft unexceptionable behaviour, and
irreproachable character, whenever the ma-
lice, animofity, or avarice of fome of the
worft of men, may inftigate them to fuch
means of gratifying thefe paffions : if this,
I fay, be really the cafe, to be liable to
fuch evils is itfelf a grievance ; a grievance
which it would be want of prudence, of regard to the welfare of thofe in whom we
are interefted, and of a juft concern for the
common caufe of liberty itfelf, not to be
folicitous to remove. To reprefent the petition of the diffenters, therefore, as a foli-
citation for what is apparently fomething,
but really nothing, [g] is, with fubmiffion to
a late writer, fcarcely confiftent with that
candor of which he makes fuch ample profeffions. And were it fo, the difficulty would
only fall back upon himfelf, and leave every
man, who is unwilling to admit unfavourable
thoughts of the juftice and humanity of his
fellow creatures, at a lofs for a reafon for
his being fo much difturbed, by the diffenters making an application for, what he
calls, an unfubftantial favour. [h] To fay, " it
" was too much to be granted, and too little
" to afk, " [i] may pleafe the imagination by
the antithefis, but has too much the air of
an enigma in it ever to fatisfy the under-
standing,

---

[g] Letter, p. 4.   [h] Ibid. p. 4.   [i] Ibid. p. 37.

ftanding. It may found prettily, but will not bear the teft of a fober examination. If the judgment of the petitioners is to determine this point; what they apprehend it reafonable to requeft, and worthy of their application to obtain, is neither too great to be granted, nor too little to be afked. If, on the other hand, the perfons, to whom the petition is addreffed, allow the requeft to be reafonable, it may be, indeed, in their opinion too little to be afked (for it fhould, in that cafe, have been given without afking) but it can never be thought too great to be granted. And fhould it be fuppofed, once more, that the requeft is deemed an unreafonable one; the contradiction ftill remains. The fubject of the requeft may, it is true, be judged too great to be granted : but then it can never be too little, but too much, abundantly too much to be afked. To confider a grant as next to nothing, and yet to oppofe it with the ferioufnefs with which this author feems to oppofe it, is, in reality, almoft without a precedent. The fmallnefs of a favour has often been deemed a good reafon for beftowing it; but it is not eafy to recollect an inftance, in which it has been judged, of itfelf, a fufficient ground for with-holding it. And were the alteration defired by the petition of the diffenters, only an apparent improvement of the Toleration,

there

there is reafon to believe, that many of the
eftablifhment, as well as the diffenters, would
fincerely rejoice to fee it adopted, as a pur-
gation of our laws from what numbers confider as fo many blemifhes in them, the taking away of which they cannot help thinking would greatly encreafe their beauty, and
give new force to that noble, and, in the
main, juft encomium of them, that the
" idea and practice of political and civil
" liberty flourifh in their higheft vigour in
" thefe kingdoms, where it falls little fhort
" of perfection." [k]   But many it feems judge
differently, and prefage that fuch an alteration would be productive of great and a-
larming evils : and it is fit that the objection fhould be impartially confidered ; for
it muft be confeffed it is a popular one,
and fuch as may ftrike forcibly on the minds
of thofe, who do not attend carefully to the
real ftate of the queftion.

It has been faid, then, that were the requeft of the diffenters to be granted, herefies would increafe, and the common faith
of chriftians be fubverted ; and therefore it
is fit, (for this muft be the meaning of the
objection) that the laws relating to diffenting
minifters fhould continue as they are.   It is
eafy to fee, that this reafoning afcribes to
the magiftrate a right of reftraining herefies,

                                                    or

of opinions which are not orthodox, by penalties, or else it proves nothing. If it is
allowed to afcribe this right to the magiftrate, it proves too much ; much more than,
I am perfuaded, thofe, who now make ufe
of it, will be difpofed to acknowledge. For,
by the very fame train of reafoning, all the
edicts of heathen governors againft chriftians,
the execution of the decrees of popes, and
councils, againft proteftants, by popifh prin-
ces, and, in a word, all perfecuting exertions
of power whatever againft thofe, who depart
from eftablifhed doctrines, might be eafily
juftified. But other alarming confequences
of complying with the defire of the diffenters are apprehended. One of their writers,
it is alledged, has charged every church
which maintains the doctrine of the TRINITY
with being *idolatrous.* ' Becaufe the diffenting
minifters inferted no offer in their bill, to
fubfcribe to the doctrine of the Trinity, it
is concluded, not by the ftricteft rules of
logick, that this is one doctrine which fome
of the petitioners defire to be at liberty to
oppofe or deny ; ᵐ — and from hence a fuppofition is formed, that there is a poffibility
" that by urging the precedent of the ido-
" latrous people of Canaan," ⁿ the hearers
of diffenting minifters may be ripened " for
" the expulfion or extermination of " the

L.   members

· Letter, p. 11.   ʳ Ibid. p. 13.   Ibid. p. 15.

members of the eftablifhment, " as an act
" of obedience to the divine command."
Diffenters, it appears, are not the only people liable to be thrown into panicks. But
to be ferious. All this is only a proof of
what has been already fuggefted; that the
petition of the diffenters has been ftrangely
mifunderftood. All, which is defired by it,
fo far as the articles are concerned, is, in
effect, this; that diffenting minifters may be
exempted from the PENALTIES, to which their
not having complied with the fubfcription
to them, required by the act of Toleration,
leaves them fubject. The words of the bill
are, " Whereas, by an act made in the 1ft
" year of the reign of King William III.
" &c. preachers or teachers of any diffent-
" ing congregations, are required, &c. to
" declare their approbation, and to fubfcribe
" the articles of religion, mentioned in the
" ftatute of the 13th of Queen Elizabeth,
" except as in the faid act, &c. is excepted;
" and whereas, many fuch perfons fcruple to
" declare their approbation of, &c. be it
" enacted, &c. that fo much of the faid
" act, &c. as relates to the faid articles, or
" to any of them, fhall be, and the fame is
" hereby repealed." ° Suppofe this had been
granted, what would have been the effect?
Would

° See the bill, at the end of Mr. Mauduit's pamphlet.

Would it have put the diſſenters into poſ-ſeſſion of any legal liberty to write or preach againſt any of the doctrines of the eſtabliſh-ment, from which they are now excluded? By no means. Not to be obliged to ſub-ſcribe to, and declare an approbation of principles, is one thing; to WRITE OR PREACH AGAINST them is another. To deſire not to lie under a load, which would cruſh the moſt humble, ſilent, and cautious diſſen-ter, as well as one of the moſt oppoſite qualities; and to aſk for a legal right to give way to thoſe *angry. indecent* invectives, to which ſome perſons ſeem to think the diſſenters ſo greatly addicted, are two points, ſo totally diſtinct, that it is ſurpriſing that gentlemen of abilities ſhould ever confound them together. The generality of diſſenting miniſters have very little inclination, I be-lieve, to conſume the time devoted to their publick inſtructions, in preaching againſt the eſtabliſhment. They have greater points in view. But had their application been ſuc-cefsful, the doctrines of the national church would have been very little, if any thing, more expoſed to ſuch attacks, than they are now it has miſcarried. It has been ſuppo-ſed[?] that the proviſo in the act of Tolera-tion, [which ſays " that nothing therein " contained ſhall extend, or be conſtrued to

L 2   " extend,

" extend, to give any eafe, &c. to any pa-
" pift, or to any perfon that fhall deny,
" in his preaching or writing, the doctrine
" of the bleffed Trinity, as it is declared in
" the aforefaid articles of religion : " ᑫ] would
have been affected if the bill in queftion
had paffed. There is room for a doubt, at
leaft, whether this claufe would have been
at all affected. ' But grant that it would ; —

pro-

ᑫ §. 17.

' It is allowed, that the expreffion in the bill, at
the end of the cafe of the diffenters, is very comprehen-
five : for it defires that fo much of the faid act, &c. as
relates to the faid articles, or to any of them, may be
repealed. And, were the expreffion to be taken fingly,
and independently of any other words, with which it
is connected, there might be fome appearance of reafon
for the application, of which the author of the letter to
the diffenting minifters, fuppofes it capable. But, if
it be confidered that it makes only the conclufion
of a fentence, in which the fcruples of the diffenting
minifters, relating to fubfcription, are affigned as the
ground of their application to parliament ; — that the
defired repeal of what relates to the articles, in the
act, has a direct reference to thofe fcruples, and is
propofed as a remedy againft the difficulties occafioned
by them : when all this is laid together, I fay, it may
furely be concluded, that the faireft and moft candid,
and indeed the moft natural interpretation of the words
is, that a repeal of fo much of the act, as relates to
a SUBSCRIPTION to the faid articles, or to any of
them, is defired. It is not, indeed, after all, of any
material confequence, which of thefe conftructions is
fuppofed to be the trueft. — However this may be determined,

profecutions for herefy, according to the notions given of it by our laws,* would have
ftood upon the fame footing, upon which
they ftand now ; — the honour of the liturgy
would have been kept under the fame protection, which now defends it ; ' — the 10th
of William III. would have retained its authority ; — in a word, all thefe guards of the
principles and worfhip of the eftablifhment,
would have fubfifted in their full vigour.
And upon what foundation then, can the
application of the diffenters be confidered as
a requeft for permiffion by law, to preach
againft the fundamental doctrines of the national church ? Or with what propriety could
the compliance of the legiflature have been
reprefented as fetting up the opinion of a
fmall body of diffenting minifters againft
the fundamental doctrines of the chriftian
church ?

termined, the doctrine of the Trinity is ftill guarded
by law, as ftrongly as can be defired. But when fur-
mifes are fubftituted inftead of certain facts ; when fuf-
picions fupply the place of proofs ; and infinuations
are introduced to play upon men's prejudices, alarm
their jealoufies, and divert their attention from the
real point in queftion ; it is fit that the requeft of the
diffenters fhould be precifely ftated, and cleared from
all thofe mifapprehenfions, which might incline perfons to think unfavourably of it, and form difadvanta-
geous judgments of thofe who promoted it.

* 1 Eliz. cap. i. §. 36.   ' 1 Eliz. cap. ii. §. 9.

church? Or what fhadow of reafon can
there be in urging the apprehenfion of one
thing, as a plea for retaining a power of punifhing perfons for another, which is utterly
different from it, and has no relation to it?
That men may have invincible objections to
fubfcription, and yet be zealous advocates for
the doctrine of the Trinity, and the doctrine
of Satisfaction too, the warmeft oppofers of
the diffenters in this affair will fcarcely deny. And by what one good political maxim
can it be juftified, to contend for leaving
room to reftrain actions by the means of
laws, which, if executed, muft bring heavy fufferings upon thofe, who never were
guilty of the offence, which, it is pretended,
makes them neceffary; and, if they are not
to be executed, muft be wholly ineffectual
to guard againft it?

The argument, which has been drawn from
this laft confideration, to fhow that a more
extenfive Toleration will not be productive
of inconveniencies, is treated, indeed, by the
author of the letter fo often cited, with fome
contempt. " But the diffenters muft beg his
pardon, if they think it merited a different
anfwer. What they advance flows with un-
deniable evidence from his own affertions;
and he muft either admit the juftice of it,
or give up all, which he has faid to fhow
the

" Letter, p. 21.

the requeſt of the diſſenters to be a needleſs
one. As long as it is but intimated, that
circumſtances may occur, in which it may
be proper to have reçourſe to the penal laws
againſt diſſenters, and the continuance of
them is contended for as neceſſary, though
they are pretended to be kept up only *in
terrorem* ; ſo long the diſſenters will have
reaſon to be alarmed. Should the execution
of them once be put in motion, none can
ſay where it will ſtop : nor may it be always
in the power of the greateſt perſons to check
its violence. If it is certain, on the other
hand, that no ſuch thing will ever be attempted, theſe laws muſt loſe all their efficacy. It is too much to be taken for
granted, that the reſtraints of law are always
of real uſe. ᵂ The reſtraints of good laws
are real bleſſings. Thoſe of bad laws are real
evils. But it is only on a ſuppoſition that they
MAY be executed, that they will be either.
Indeed for this gentleman to imagine that
keeping up an obligation to ſubſcribe, when,
by his own confeſſion, " that part of the law,
[which requires it] " is now as dead as if the
" whole law were obſolete " ˣ can have any
great influence upon the mode of thinking
and ſpeaking, of which ſuch terrible apprehenſions are entertained, is utterly miſtaking
the true ſource of it. For it is not the dif-
uſe

ᵂ Letter, p. 21.   ˣ Ibid. p. 37.

use of subscription, which has produced this freedom of thought and language upon religious subjects; but it is this freedom of thought, which has produced the disuse of subscription. Taking away the obligation to subscribe would make very little alteration in the case. If this liberty of speech should afterwards encrease, the change in the law would be so far from deserving to be thought the proper cause, that it could scarcely be thought, with justice, to be the remote occasion of this increase. The real causes would continue to be the same, which they ever have been; the growth of an inquisitive disposition; and the advancement of that largeness of mind, which invites persons to propose their sentiments freely; makes the exertion of the civil power, on account of difference in opinions, odious; and, thus checks the operation of those laws which, in times of another complexion, would be carried into rigorous execution.

But admit that, to adopt the language which has been used on this occasion, heresies might abound something more; is keeping up penal laws the proper remedy against them? Is this a competent reason for refusing the dissenters that liberty, which, upon all the just principles of Toleration, they are entitled to enjoy? For to these principles, after all, the appeal must be made; and if

they

they are again brought before the mind of the reader, the repetition, cannot, with reafon, be blamed. Gentlemen who know not how to difpute their truth, and yet are unwilling to admit their plain confequences, may, to evade the force of them, be in hafte to fay, " 'tis needlefs to urge them ; they are " admitted ; but they are mifapplied." But when all, which is owned to be indifputable in the right of private judgment, (which has generally been thought to include a right of publick worſhip, according to that judgment) feems to be reduced ʸ to the bare poffeffion of that inward conviction, to which " no power of government can extend," and for which it is needlefs to fupplicate even " in an arbitrary ftate ; " is there not a caufe to have recourfe to them ? When defiring not to be criminals in the eye of the ftate, till fome real offence againſt that ftate, (which not profeffing an agreement with the articles of the national church can never be,) is proved upon them : when this, I fay, is unfairly confounded with " a pretended right to ex- " empt certain publick acts, " univerfally, (for this word muft be underſtood, though it is not expreffed,) from the cognizance of the civil power ; can inculcating the principles of Toleration, in thefe circumſtances, with any reafon be thought needlefs ? If the

M   right

ʸ Letter, p. 24, 25.

right of the governors of the ſtate, or of the church, to " prevent the opinions of private " men from claſhing with ſuch of the eſta- " bliſhed doctrines as are fundamental ; " [z] that is (for this is, in fact, the caſe) which they think fundamental, " ſo long as it can be " done without violence ; " if this, I ſay, be urged as a plea for continuing laws in force, which, if they operate at all, muſt have ſome degree of violence in their operation : every man is left to judge, whether to lead the thoughts of men back to the true grounds of religious liberty, does not become highly neceſſary. Nor can it, with any rea- ſon, be ſaid, they are miſapplied, [a] The ſafety of the ſtate, and the principles of Toleration, · it is allowed, are in perfect conſiſtence with each other. The bounda- ries, which determine the right exerciſe of power on the one hand, and of liberty on the other, are to be marked out with an impartial view to both theſe important points. But the ſafety of the ſtate can never be rightly pretended as a reaſon for laws in- conſiſtent with the clear dictates of juſtice and humanity. And that the ſafety of the ſtate is at all concerned in ſubſcription to a number of articles, ſome of which are owned to be ſuperfluous, [b] to have been in- ſerted to reconcile the predeceſſors of the
diſſenters

---

[z] Letter, p. 28.   [a] Ibid. p. 18.   [b] Ibid. p. 26.

diffenters to the church, and are now not
confidered as important; the diffenters never
did admit, neither do they yet admit it. They
think they may add, with reafon, that the
largeft degree of Toleration which they have
folicited, carries nothing in it ᶜ incompatible with any fecurity, which the eftablifhed
church can equitably defire; and believe,
that if they declare they cannot yet fee the
manifeft impropriety of their requeft, ᵈ it
will be no impeachment of their underftanding.

Whether the general character and deportment of the diffenters have given any juft occafion for them to be efteemed unworthy of
the liberty which they have afked, is chearfully left to the judgment of all who are difpofed to judge candidly. Their loyalty has
been acknowledged in the moft publick manner. With refpect to their zeal for liberty,
and the fupport of the conftitution, if we are
rightly informed, they have been honoured
with the fingular, and perhaps not wholly
unmerited applaufe, of having been, in fome
feafons, almoft the only fteadfaft adherents
to that glorious caufe. For their zeal for
the honour of chriftianity, and their merits
as advocates, in behalf of it, they prefume
they may chearfully turn themfelves to the
reverend the clergy of all orders, as their

M 2

fa-

favourable judges. From the same respectable body, they doubt not but they may hope to receive an honourable testimony to the application, learning and sagacity, with which many among them have devoted their abilities to the illustration of the sacred writings. It has been urged against them, that they are an intolerant sect. They own, without hesitation, that time was when too many, who passed under their denomination, were justly chargeable with this spirit; and, with as little hesitation they confess, it was a reproach to their predecessors that they were so. But it was the common error of the age. Numbers of their brethren of the establishment, were once liable to the same objection. But they have, in general, renounced their error, and think their assurances of this ought to be believed. The dissenters have long since, and universally, done the same; and hope they may, with equal reason, expect to have credit given them for the truth and reality of their repentance. For reasons, which have often been laid before the world, they decline constant and entire conformity to the worship of the established church; but the justice, which they have been always ready to do to the writings of her members, and to the piety, learning, and eminent attainments of her clergy; the zeal and resolution, with which

they

they have, in very criticial and hazardous seasons, joined with their fellow subjects, in withstanding attempts, which were made for her destruction; and the self-denying steadfastness, with which they have refused to concur in measures, which they apprehended were concerted with designs unfriendly to their protestant brethren, even at a time, when too many of those brethren discovered not the kindest disposition to them: all these are convincing tokens, that though they dissent, they do it not only with charity, but with high esteem. The general tenor of their deportment, towards the clergy and laity of the national church, they presume, gives a new proof of their being filled with these sentiments. Let it not be said, they make a merit of this. They take a pleasure in owning, that great numbers of their brethren of the establishment, and those, persons of rank and eminence, have given them a pattern of moderation and gentleness, which it was their duty and praise to imitate, and treated them with an affability and good nature, sufficient to make impressions on hearts, far less susceptible of friendly sentiments than those, which, it is hoped, are commonly lodged in the bosoms of dissenters. But this may be said with great truth, that the dissenters have had no example of this kind set before them, but

what

what they have been earneftly defirous to
follow; and have received no marks of benevolence and friendfhip, but what they
have always been folicitous to return, in the
moft ample manner, which has been in their
power. And though, from their late application to parliament, occafion has been taken to introduce oblique charges of viru-
lence and hatred; ° and the relief, which
they afked, has had the furprizing complaint
made of it; f that it " could only anfwer
" the purpofe of manifefting to the world,"
that they " were indifpofed to tolerate" their
brethren, " as an eftablifhment : " they deferve to have a much milder fentence paffed upon them. Their minifters, in particular, upon whom thefe intimations are like
chiefly to fall, are men of a better fpirit :
men, who would have rejoiced to clofe
breaches, rather than to widen them; and
who, when they have reflected upon the
character of many of the clergy, whofe abilities they efteem, whofe learning they value,
and whofe virtues they honour, have filently
lamented, that there fhould be fuch a wall
of partition remaining, to keep them and
their brethren afunder. They have the fatisfaction to obferve, that the gentleman himfelf, from whom thefe expreffions are taken,
in other parts of his pamphlet, fpeaks in
                                        milder

° Letter, p. 56, 58.   f Ibid. p. 38.

milder terms of them. He owns, indeed, the MERIT of several among them, with a politenefs, which entitles him to their moft refpectful acknowledgments; and makes it rather furprizing how difpofitions fo oppo-fite to thofe, which really influence them, and views fo diftant from thofe, which were the true fprings of their application, could be imputed to them.

One thing more remains to be confidered; which is, the declaration which the diffenters offered, inftead of the fubfcription, now re-quired by law. And forry I am that there fhould be any occafion to vindicate this from objections; and much pleafure would it have given me to have fpared fome animadver-fions, which, by the exceptions made to this part of their conduct, are rendered unavoidable. The declaration, as it ftands in the bill, prepared for the relief of the diffenters, is this. *I, A. B. do declare, as in the prefence of Almighty God, that I believe that the Scriptures of the Old and New Tefta-ment contain a revelation of the mind and will of God; and that I receive them as the rule of my faith and practice.* ᵍ The reflections which the author of the letter to the dif-fenting minifters makes, upon this declara-tion, are thefe. " You offer to fubfcribe to " the Holy Scriptures, as containing a re-
" velation

ᵍ The cafe of the diffenters, p. 60, 61.

" velation of the mind and will of God,
" and being the rule of your faith and
" practice. You know full well, gentlemen,
" that there is not an error, however ob-
" noxious to christians, or however subverfive
" of civil fociety, which may not be cover-
" ed, under the cloak of this fubfcription.
" Need I tell you, that tranfubstantiation,
" purgatory, invocation of faints, idolatry,
" murthers, rebellions, and almoft every evil
" work, have been drawn from mifinterpre-
" tations of fcripture? Had you refufed *all*
" fubfcription, the ftate had been full as
" fecure as in the offer of one fo very un-
" fatisfactory and indeterminate. It had,
" really, the appearance of trifling with the
" legiflature, which, as you could not intend
" it, had, at beft, the appearance of pre-
" fuming upon their total inattention to mat-
" ters of this fort, or upon their taking
" them very fuperficially into confiderati-
" on." [b]

In the twenty-eighth page of this pamphlet, " an eminent writer " among the diffenters, is charged with carrying his idea of
liberty, quite to a fhocking extreme. Shock-
ing is a ftrong term, and were it to be returned upon this gentleman, on account of
the length to which he is carried, by his
zeal for fubfcription to human articles, he
might

---

[a] Letter, p. 10, 11.

might poffibly complain. But certainly it
may be faid, that he has, in this paffage,
made ufe of expreffions, which the calmeft,
moft difpaffionate perfon, cannot read without EMOTION. Could it have been expected,
indeed, that an author, whofe performance
expreffes fo much of a concern for chriftianity and proteftantifm, would have allowed
himfelf in fuch degrading language as this,
concerning a folemn declaration of cordial
affent, to the whole body of the facred writings? Is that doctrine, which is according
to godlinefs; [i] that fcripture which the
apoftle declares, to be " profitable for doc-
" trine, for reproof, for correction, for in-
" ftruction in righteoufnefs, that the man of
" God may be perfect, thoroughly furnifhed
" unto all good works," [k] fo loofe, defective and indeterminate, " that there is not
an error, how obnoxious foever, or however
fubverfive of civil fociety, but what may be
covered under the cloak of fubfcription to
it?" [l] When it is the acknowledged defign
of the whole tenor of the books of the Old
and New Teftament, to eftablifh the worfhip
of the only living and true God, and to
teach men to deny all ungodlinefs and worldly
lufts: [m] can the ferious profeffion of our
owning them, as the rule of our faith and

N   practice,

[i] 1 Tim. vi. 3.　[k] 2 Tim. iii. 16.
[l] Letter, p. 10, 11.　[m] Titus. ii. 12

practice, be juftly fuppofed to contain in it, no affurance of the orderly, virtuous deportment of thofe who make it ? When we find this revelation of the will of God declaring, in the moft expreffive terms, that neither idolaters, nor adulterers, nor thieves, nor drunkards, nor revilers, nor extortioners, fhall inherit the kingdom of God ; is the language of it fo indeterminate and void of force, that it places no effectual guard againft thofe enormities ? Becaufe it may have happened, that tranfubftantiation, purgatory, invocation of faints, idolatry, and other errors and evil works, have been fheltered under mifinterpretations of fcripture ; are the words of it to be fuppofed fo deftitute of clearnefs and precifion, as to give no fufficient pledge to government, for the good behaviour of thofe who own their divine authority ? Or would the refufal of *all* fubfcription, which might have left it uncertain whether perfons acknowledged any religion at all, have made the ftate full as fecure as the profeffion of thofe principles, which carry in them every awful reftraint from evil, and every powerful motive to good actions, which can be prefented to the human mind ? If this declaration is not an adequate fatisfaction to the legiflature, what fatisfaction can the fubfcription required by the act of Toleration be ? Men of frantick, enthufiaftick minds, may abufe

every

every thing. Men of difhoneft and infin-
cere hearts. may, and will, fubfcribe any
thing; take any oaths, conform to any teft,
which human policy can invent: and no
articles, were they to be diverfified and adjufted to the exigencies of the times ever
fo often, and encreafed till they equalled the
moft voluminous confeffion, which ever exifted, will be fufficient to bind them. All
thefe fecurities muft imply common fenfe and
integrity, in thofe who give them, to make
them of the leaft avail: and if this gentleman allows, as he profeffes to do, (and, I
doubt not, with fincerity,) that the petitioning
minifters have fome right not to be accounted deftitute of either of thefe qualities; he
will, it is hoped, upon fecond thoughts acknowledge, that the fecurity, which they offered, in their propofed declaration, was neither trifling nor fallacious; but as determinate and perfectly adapted to prevent every
doubt, which the rulers of a ftate can reafonably entertain, as any of which they could
poffibly have made a tender. The legiflature
has indeed already, in effect, accepted it as
fufficient, in the cafe of the quakers; for
excepting the eftablifhed doctrine of the
Trinity, (which, however true it may be in
itfelf, and how important foever in a theo-
logical view, makes the reftraints of the gofpel upon immorality and difobedience to go-

vernment, no more precife and determinate
than the arian or focinian doctrine of it;)
they are only required to profefs their belief
in the infpiration of the fcriptures. And, if
the ftate be fecured by this declaration from
them, why fhould more be neceffary for this
purpofe from other proteftant diffenters ? [n]

To

[o] If this writer fhould fay, that by giving fatisfaction to the ftate, he means declaring an approbation of fuch merely religious opinions, as the government has thought fit to take into the national
church, he has expreffed himfelf ambiguoufly, and not
very properly. All, which is underftood by fecurity
to the ftate, in the common acceptation of the words,
and all, which the ftate can, in reafon require, is,
fufficient affurance that men will behave as peaceable
members of fociety, " pay tribute to whom tribute,
" cuftom to whom cuftom, fear to whom fear, and
" honour to whom honour is due;" and be faithful
and bear true allegiance to thofe, who rule over them.
But there is a much greater imperfection than mere
impropriety, in making an affent to the doctrines of
an eftablifhment a neceffary part of the fatisfaction
due to the ftate; for it implies, that the magiftrate
has a right to enforce his own fenfe of fcripture, by
penalties, on thofe, who do not acquiefce in it. Whether this be the meaning of this author I will not
pretend to affirm; but it ought not to be his meaning. A writer, who has expreffed himfelf with fuch
laudable indignation, againft the fhare, which Calvin
had in the death of Servetus, has not left himfelf at
liberty to be an advocate for reftraining a diffent, from
the eftablifhed faith, even by the fmalleft punifhments;
which a fpirit of perfecution will always be ready to
change into greater, till it has accomplifhed the de-
ftruction of all, which ftands in the way of its fury.

To employ many words in refuting other objections against this declaration, such as, that it might be made by heathens, deifts, or mahometans, (and jews might as well have been added to the lift,) would be little better than trifling with the time of the reader. To acknowledge, that the facred scriptures not only contain a revelation of the will of God, but that they are to be received as THE RULE of faith and practice, plainly implies, not barely that they contain truth, but fo far as it is to be learnt, from revelation only, ALL truth which we are bound to receive on the authority of it. The obvious force of the expreffion is, not only that the Old and New Teftament are a ftandard, by which truth and error are to be judged, but that they are the only fupernatural ftandard, to which we are to have recourfe, for this purpofe. And how totally repugnant this is, to the principles of thofe who reject all revelation; of thofe, who admit the authority of Mofes, but reject that of Jefus; or of thofe, who admit the divine miffion of Jefus, but fuperfede his Gofpel, by introducing the pretended miffion of Mahomet, and contending for the Koran, as the rule of faith and practice; is too plain to need enlargement. He indeed, who does not difcern it of himfelf, will fcarcely difcern it by the help of any arguments which can be of-

fered

fered to him. The declaration, fairly inter-
preted, equally implies the great principles of
the Reformation, and is utterly inconfiftent
with thofe of Popery ; and, whatever fufpici-
ons might be entertained, from the compre-
henfive nature of it, by fome perfons ; yet if
the affair be impartially confidered, it will be
found the only one, which, without coun-
teracting their own views, and the avowed principles of their denomination, they
could propofe. The diffenters, it is well
known, though not more widely diftant from
each other, than many of thofe who, in the
eftablifhed church, are acknowledged as her
members, admitted to her communion, and
advanced to the higheft preferments ; are very
far from being uniform in their fentiments,
concerning the controverted points of divi-
nity. To have drawn up, and offered particular fubfcriptions, relating to any of thefe,
therefore, would have been excluding many
of themfelves from the benefit defired.
Could they have agreed in a confeffion, in
which the majority would have united ; to
have folicited relief only upon that footing,
would have been grofly and indefenfibly
partial. It would have been leaving the burthen, and that probably with much aggravated
weight, upon others, whom, how far foever
they may be from adopting fome of their tenets, they think to have an equal right, upon

on every equitable principle, to Toleration
with themselves. But, above all, it would
have been departing from that fundamental
maxim, upon which they are proteftants and
diffenters, and, by adhering to which, they
think they fhall beft ferve the caufe of real
chriftianity; that the words of God, and not
the explications of fallible men, are the authentick tefts of truth and orthodoxy. They
thought themfelves bound therefore, to offer
no fubfcription, but to the facred writings;
and laudably fetting afide all their internal
diftinctions, agreed in this, as the only confiftent and catholick principle, upon which
their caufe could be refted.

Catholick and charitable, however, as their
conduct to each other may appear; it is
charged with difcovering a different fpirit,
towards thofe of the eftablifhment. It is
reprefented as confidering the confeffion of
faith of the church of England, " as a
" yoke or a burthen, too heavy to be borne
" by proteftants." ° To intimate this is apprehended to have a manifeft tendency to
" diffolve the proteftant union; and the
" time, it is faid may come, when the dif-
" fenters will not regret, that they are ac-
" knowledged by law, as members of the
" proteftant church." Do the remonftrants,
in Holland, then, diffolve the proteftant union,

on, by rejecting some articles of the Belgick confeſſion ? Or are they conſidered by the ſtates, as no part of the proteſtant church, becauſe they are now diſſenters, in points of doctrine, from the eſtabliſhed church of that republick ? With ſubmiſſion to this gentleman's better acquaintance with theſe things, it is apprenended that *true* proteſtantiſm, and an attachment to SCRIPTURAL chriſtianity, are the ſame thing ; that to maintain the ſufficiency and perfection of ſcripture, is what properly conſtitutes a proteſtant ; that the agreement of thoſe who firſt bore the name, in ſeveral points which were maintained by the firſt reformers, was merely accidental to the character ; and that all, who aſſent to the inſpired writings, as the only rule by which chriſtians are to be bound, retain their title to this honourable name. And, the more cloſely they adhere to theſe ſacred oracles, and the more carefully they bring all confeſſions and ſyſtems of opinions to them, as the touchſtone, by which the value of all human deciſions in religion is to be aſcertained, the more conſiſtently and perfectly proteſtant their behaviour deſerves to be accounted.

But it is not only with a kind of apoſtacy from proteſtantiſm, but want of a friendly ſpirit to the eſtabliſhment, that the diſſenters are charged for their late attempt. Succeſs

in

in it, we are told, [p] would have " been but
" the poor femblance of a triumph ; " perfift-
ing in the attempt will be a caufe, it is
faid, for confidering the diffenting minifters
as men, who " to make their hatred to the
" eftablifhment more effectual, are ready to
" feize upon every favourable time and op-
" portunity of manifefting it." [q]   The application is taxed again, for it feems to be
a favourable topick, with " implying a defire
" to make a reconciliation more defperate
" than ever : " [r]   and granting the requeft,
it is afferted, would have been declaring by
a " new law, that the bond of union, " between " his Majefty's proteftant fubjects,
" who are fuppofed by law to maintain the
" fame chriftian doctrines, is broken. " [s]   Perfons of ability and refinement, may ftrike
many meanings out of any meafure, which
never entered into the hearts of thofe who
engaged in it. But this meafure authorizes
no fuch conftruction. It implies, it is true,
that the prefent diffenters have objections to
fubfcribing to fome of the articles, which
their predeceffors had not. But this has been
long known ; and petitioning not to be fubject to penalties, on that account, makes not
the leaft alteration in the cafe ; nor had the
petition been granted, would it in the leaft

O   have

---

[p] Letter, p. 41.   [q] Ibid. p. 58.   [r] Ibid. p. 38.

[s] Ibid. p. 22.

have leſſened the ties of affection, by which, it is hoped, thoſe, who are of the eſtabliſhment, and thoſe, who diſſent from it, would ſtill have been bound to each other, as thoſe who are " of the ſame body, and partakers of the " ſame promiſe in Chriſt, by the goſpel." But let the caſe be as this gentleman has ſtated it. What has rejecting the petition done towards preſerving this union, for which he profeſſes himſelf ſo ſolicitous ? It cannot be ſuppoſed to bring the JUDGMENT of the diſſenters a ſtep nearer to the articles than they were before ; and all thought of compelling perſons to expreſs their approbation of them, contrary to their judgment, is what he utterly diſclaims. Had the bill paſſed, it would have been a noble addition to the proofs, which the church of England has given of her moderation to diſſenting proteſtants ; and had the fathers of the church been zealous in promoting it, they would have erected MONUMENTUM AERE PERENNIUS to their praiſe. But rejecting the bill, has rather the appearance of excluding thoſe, who decline ſubſcription, from the number of thoſe whom the eſtabliſhment chooſes to acknowledge as brethren. Inſtead of diſcovering an unwillingneſs to part with them, it looks much more like a readineſs to caſt them off, as unfit to be comprehended in that legal protection, which they were moved to ſeek, by no other

principles

principles than a regard to their own fafety, and to the caufe of liberty; and, on their application for which, a defire to fhow the leaft hoftile difpofitions to the members of the eftablifhment, had not the remoteft influence.

So far, in reality, are the diffenters in general, from being actuated by fuch motives as thefe, that the very reverfe of this is the truth. Senfible and moderate men, both in the eftablifhment and out of it, feem to be gradually moving on to a more open and friendly intercourfe with each other. — Their fentiments on points which were formerly the fubject of much and warm controverfy, more generally coincide. — The diftinction between the great end and effentials of religion, and the mere circumftantials which attend it, is better underftood and more generally acknowledged. But it unhappily falls out, that the nearer the diffenters approach in fome of thefe things, to a great part of the members of the eftablifhment, to the greater diftance they find themfelves removed from fome of the articles of it. The lefs diflike fome among them may retain to the mode of the publick fervices of the church, the greater objections they have to fome of the materials, which are incorporated with them; and thus, while fome circumftances might feem to prepare the way for a more

perfect

perfect union, there are others, which, as things are now fettled, raife up new and ftill ftronger obftacles to it : obftacles, which not even the example and authority of the great CHILLINGWORTH,[t] will enable them to furmount. The diffenters have always held the memory of that eminent man in the jufteft veneration. They think of him with peculiar fatisfaction, for the noble and fuccefsful ardour, with which he afferted the fole right and authority of the facred fcriptures to command the affent and fubmiffion of chriftians : but they cannot implicitly give themfelves up to his judgment, and follow his example contrary to their fentiments. His practice, indeed, if we may credit the account given of his fubicription, by hands, which appear to be good, bears no fuch teftimony to the articles as feems to be collected from it. His own fenfe of it, as we are told by the author of his life, is expreffed in thefe words : " I do verily " believe the church of England a true " member of the church catholick ; that fhe " wants nothing neceffary to falvation, and " holds nothing repugnant thereto." " And " I thought (he adds) that to think fo, had " fufficiently qualified me for a fubicripti- " on."[u] Were this all, which is intended

by

[t] Letter, p. 52.
[u] Free and candid Difquifit. p. 169. ed. 1749.

by subscription, the dissenters would have much less objection to it than they have; and it is reasonable to believe this application to parliament would never have been heard of. But by what competent authority has this ever been determined? Bishop Burnet [w] supposes indeed, that this is all, which is implied in the communion of the laity with the church; but, desirous as he was to soften the hard injunction of subscription, against which he left his dying testimony, [x] he could not apply it to the declaration required of the clergy. I think it may be justly doubted, whether this author himself will admit of this sense of subscription. Expounded in this manner, it carries nothing more in it than what arians, socinians, or in a word any, who reject those articles of the church, which he considers as fundamental, may subscribe, if they have but charity sufficient to acknowledge the belief of them consistent with salvation. And with what justice then could he imagine that the example of a person, who is believed to have subscribed only in this meaning, could be of any force to remove the scruples of the dissenters concerning it?

Indeed till this gentleman, or some other of the zealous advocates for subscription,

have

---

[w] Exposit. of the articles, p. 6. ed. 1720.

[x] Conclusion of his hist. p. 624. vol. ii. folio ed.

have more precisely determined the meaning
and extent of it, the doubts, not only of
thofe out of the eftablifhment, but of numbers of thoughtful perfons in it, will continue in all their ftrength. From the ftrefs
laid upon it, by this writer at leaft, which
is fo great that he treats releafing the diffenters from it, as an indulgence which might
have been pernicious to the ftate,[y] (and by
which, the chriftian religion itfelf might have
been affected,[z]) fuch as are unacquainted with
what has been faid upon the fubject, might be
led to fuppofe that the import of it was out
of all difpute, and that it was allowed to be
an indifputable affurance of affection to the
doctrines of the articles. And yet there is
fcarcely a point more controverted. Some
contend earneftly, that hearty affent to them,
in the fenfe of the compilers, is the neceffary meaning of it; and confider fubfcribing, in
any other fenfe, as incapable of vindication.
— Other gentlemen, of great learning, think
themfelves warranted in fubfcribing with
greater latitude. — Others have been defirous
to confider the articles as articles of peace;
and others may have views of the matter
different from all thefe. While thefe difputes
are left undecided, what great fecurity can
fubfcriptions give to any church of the found-
nefs of its minifters? While there is fuch a
diverfity

[y] Letter, p. 58.   [z] Ibid. p. 22.

diverfity of opinions concerning the very act,
which is required in order to prevent it;
who can wonder that the diffenters choofe
to decline it, left they fhould have conftructions put upon their conduct which they cannot admit, and from which they may be
urged with conceffions, which they cannot allow themfelves to make? And they have
the pleafure to fee, that, however the practice
of the above mentioned eminent defender of
the proteftant caufe may be quoted againft
them, his principles may be quoted, and
fpeak forcibly, very forcibly, for them : and
fully juftify the fubfcription they propofed.
So long as that memorable fentence ftands
in his incomparable book ; the BIBLE, the
BIBLE only is the religion of proteftants,
the diffenters will think they have a right
to glory in him, as a patron of their caufe
in their late application : efpecially when
they join with it that noble motion of his,
which is more appofite ftill to their purpofe : " Let all men believe the fcripture,
" and that only ; and endeavour to believe
" it in the true fenfe, and require no more
" of others ; and they fhall find this a bet-
" ter means not only to fupprefs herefy, but
" to reftore unity. For he that believes the
" fcripture fincerely, and endeavours to be-
" lieve it in the true fenfe, cannot poffibly
" be an heretick. And if no more than
                                    " this

" this was required of any man, to make
" him capable of the church's communion,
" then all men so qualified, though they
" were different in opinion, yet, notwith-
" standing any such difference, they muſt
" be, of neceſſity, one in communion. " [a]

Whether there be any reaſon to expect,
that by any ſchemes, which may now, or
ſome time hence, be in contemplation, ſuch [b]
a change will be effected in our eſtabliſhment,
as will open the doors of it wide enough
for good men of all parties, to enter into
it; the diſſenters pretend not to be maſters
of ſufficient intelligence to determine. It
gives them great pleaſure to have but HINTS
from gentlemen, who appear to ſpeak from
authentick information, that ſuch a deſign is
ſeriouſly entertained. What they have heard
ſome of great eminence have ſaid muſt be
done, they flatter themſelves, ſome time will
be done. But if a century, and perhaps
much more than a century, from the laſt
ſettlement of the church, muſt intervene before ſo much as one ſtep, which can be
ſaid to have produced any effect, is taken
in this good work; if, after ſuch a ſtep is
taken, it ſhould be found inſufficient to anſwer the deſired end, and another period of
equal duration muſt complete its round before

<hr/>

[a] Concluſion of his preface, to the anthor of charity
maintained.   [b] Letter, p. 47, 59.

fore a fecond will be found admiffible, not only Dr. Furneaux, but others may doubt, without reprobating the eftablifhment as unworthy of them, whether they fhall live to fee the time when they can have the fatisfaction of being comprehended in it. Should fuch a day open upon them, I am fatisfied the diffenters will not be indifpofed to make every due acknowledgment to the wifdom and piety of the gentlemen, who quickened the approach of it. In the mean time, why fhould it be thought fo reftlefs in them to be willing to be fecured ? Or what obftruction can their attempt, in reafon, create to the defirable undertaking? Had it fucceeded, it would have put no new difficulties in the way of conformity, as the terms of it now ftand ; and fhould thofe, which as yet fubfift, be removed, refufing the diffenters their requeft, makes their way into the church no eafier, nor can it render their minds at all more difpofed to it, than if their defire had been granted. But there is one confideration more, which has great weight with the diffenters, and which they beg leave to recommend to the moft ferious thoughts of all, who undertake to judge of their conduct. They have propofed fubfcription to the Bible as a qualification, upon which they wifh to enjoy the advantages of Toleration. If the conductors of any defign, for leffening

P   the

the difficulties of the clergy, and bringing in the diffenters, fhould entertain the fame unfavourable opinion of this fubfcription, which the author of the letter, fo frequently mentioned, appears to entertain of it; [c] there is no ground to fuppofe that any alterations will fix the admiffion of minifters into the church, upon this extenfive principle: and if not, there is room to believe, that fome good, very good men, may ftill be kept out. All thofe who are fhut out from fuch an eftablifhment, will moft affuredly be fhut out from the benefit of Toleration, as it is now bounded by law. " And fhould Toleration " itfelf affume a new form, in confequence " of any change in the eftablifhment; yet, " if fubfcription to this new fet of articles " fhould be the condition of it, numbers may " ftill be deprived of all advantage from it;" for whofe fafety, therefore, fome provifion will be neceffary, and whofe cafe will be highly worthy of regard. [d] Since, inconfiderable as they may be efteemed on account of their circumftances, and, unpopular as they may be made by their fingularity; they may, neverthelefs, be fome of the moft truly con-
                                                    fcientious,

[c] Letter, p. 10, 11.
    [d] For fo much of the above fentence as is marked with commas, and which was added while the fheets of the firft edition of this effay were printing off, the author is indebted to the hint given by Dr. Kippis, p. 81. 1ft edit.

fcientious, and greatly virtuous men in the kingdom; and it can never be fit, that the peace of perfons of this charac‑ ter, fhould lie at the mercy of bigotry, ha‑ tred, or perhaps of ftill meaner princi‑ ples. Let the prefent days be ever fo mild and gentle, yet, if, in the rotation of human events, it is fuppofable that the diffent‑ ers may become the eftablifhed church; [c] it is furely equally poffible, and much lefs im‑ probable, that, in the courfe of the fame rotation, events may happen in fome diftant times, which may raife the fpirit of perfe‑ cution again among us, and bring on a re‑ petition of the feverities and fufferings of the former days. And though the prefent diffenters may be ever fo eafy for them‑ felves; yet, as the friends of mankind, and thofe who confine not their views to the prefent generation, but look forward to the poffible cafe of pofterity; they think them‑ felves juftified in their endeavours to enlarge the legal bounds of Toleration, and promote a nearer advancement of them to the extent of that juft and reafonable liberty, which, at prefent, prevails, with general approbation, in practice. And if it is allowed to be fit to prevail in practice, what good reafon can be given, for which it fhould not alfo prevail in the language of law?

P 2 The

---

[c] Letter, p. 27.

The matter indeed is reduced to this fhort and plain iffue. Either the juft principles of Toleration muft be facrificed; or the laws, from which the diffenters defire to be fheltered, muft be allowed to be indefenfible. The truth of the one, and the juftice of the other, cannot ftand together. If one of thefe oppofites muft be parted with, it is eafy to fee which is the better, more chriftian choice. And could the author of this pamphlet imagine, that it would ever rife to the notice of thofe in fuperior rank; he would beg leave, with all the deference which becomes him, to fubmit it to their ferious confideration, whether, as it is a matter of confcience with them not haftily to ADMIT requefts for the extenfion of religious liberty; it ought not alfo to be matter of confcience not caufelefsly to reject them. In the nervous language of a late prelate, of diftinguifhed eminence, " if it is not very " right to punifh men for their opinions ; " there is no medium ; it muft be very " wrong. " ᶠ The ftatutes, which authorize fuch a practice, muft be fubject to the fame alternative. If they are not very JUST, they muft be very UNJUST. And if this be their only true denomination, it can fcarcely bear a doubt, what ought to be determined concerning

---

ᶠ Difficulties and difcouragements which attend the ftudy of the fcriptures, p. 25. 9th edit.

cerning them. Certainly it can never be unworthy of the equity, clemency and wifdom of government, to fhut the door which is ftill left open for their being made inftruments of oppreffion; and entirely take away the power, which they ALWAYS GIVE, and the temptations, which they may SOME TIME OFFER, to perfons of bad difpofitions, to injure men of integrity, virtue and piety.

Whether fuch an happy alteration, with refpect to thefe laws, will be the confequence of the farther attempt, which the diffenters are now making to obtain it; they muft leave to the wifdom of the great council of the kingdom, (to whom their defires are again, with all deference, fubmitted) to determine. And, if the diffenters humbly apprehend, that there is no impropriety in the repetition of their requeft; what is there culpable in this apprehenfion? So far as the fenfe of the legiflature was concerned, the queftion was left undecided; and, upon all the principles of reafon and equity, there was ample room left for them to apply for a rehearing of their caufe. The honourable houfe of Commons allowed the juftice of their requeft; and bore teftimony to it in a manner, which will remain an evidence in favour of it, as long as the memory of the tranfactions of parliament fhall endure. Nor can it, they apprehend, be deemed an inftance of the leaft want of that
regard

regard, which they always defire to retain for that illuftrious affembly, in which their petition was not viewed in the fame advantageous light; that the diffenters, a fecond time, prefume to fubmit their requeft to the noble perfons, who before rejected it, with full reliance on their willingnefs again to honour it with their impartial, deliberate attention. Among fuch as, inftead of bringing law to reafon, bring reafon to law, and haftily conclude, that whatever is done legally, is done juftly; the diffenters are fenfible they may have many prejudices raifed againft them. But this age and kingdom abound with perfons, who are placed far above the reach of all fuch impreffions; " who are men of re-
" fined and exalted underftandings, who have
" a large compafs of thought, and have
" looked into the principles of things. Thefe
" know, that written laws are but deducti-
" ons from the law of nature, which is prior
" to all human inftitutions; that thefe fome-
" times deviate from that unwritten law;
" and, when they do, are of no real, intrin-
" fick authority. They know, that a thing
" is not juft and reafonable, becaufe it is
" enacted; but, in good governments, is
" enacted becaufe it is juft and reafonable." [h]
And it is with great fatisfaction that the
dif-

---

[h] Difficulties and difcouragements, &c. p. 25. 6th edit.

diffenters reflect, that it is before persons of this clafs that the caufe, which they have fo much at heart, is to be reviewed. With men of this truly elevated fpirit, they may juftly hope they fhall obtain a candid audience ; and they cannot but be confirmed in the hope, when they turn their thoughts to that truly refpectable band of worthies, who have, already, in this queftion, rifen up and avowed their caufe : perfons, great in their rank, and by the trufts repofed in them ; great in their abilities, and the reputation, with which they have filled up high and important ftations : but great above all in this, that, though connected by no ties of party, nor united by any views of intereft ; yet, when the venerable form of truth appears before them, they with one accord refort to her, and range themfelves under her banners. Many fuch, the diffenters are fatisfied, there are alfo among thofe, who were not inclinable, when this affair was firft propofed, to favour their caufe : nor can they relinquifh the hopes, which they entertained, that, when once thofe fears were fubfided, and thofe mifapprehenfions removed, which prevented the real ftate of their cafe from being feen in its true light ; they fhould have the pleafure and honour of numbering thefe truly refpectable perfons among their friends alfo. But, however thefe hopes may

be

be anfwered, or difappointed; there is one fatisfaction, which they will always enjoy; that the views, by which they are animated, are fuch as, inftead of deferving to be condemned, are worthy to be applauded. It is not the intereft of a party; but of chriftian liberty, truth, and charity, which they are labouring to ferve; and, however fome perfons may attempt to fet thefe interefts at variance, nothing is more certain than, that they will all be found ultimately to coincide with each other; and that the greater regard is paid to each, in its feafon, the fwifter advances will be made, to that defirable iffue, which is the hope, and wifh of the diffenters, (and in which every good heart will concur with them,) that BROTHERLY LOVE MAY CONTINUE; that all thofe remains of jealoufy, which have often defeated noble defigns, for promoting the caufe of truth and peace, may be more completely taken away; that zeal for the advancement of genuine chriftianity may temper all inferior views; and that all may increafe in their defire, with ONE HEART AND ONE MOUTH, TO GLORIFY GOD, EVEN THE FATHER OF OUR LORD JESUS CHRIST.

APPEN-

A P P E N D I X.

IN the courſe of writing the foregoing
Treatiſe, ſeveral points occurred to the
Author beſides thoſe conſidered in it, *upon* which,
though they appeared to him not unworthy
of attention, he did not then chooſe to enlarge. Farther thoughts upon the ſubject
having led him to alter his judgment, in
this reſpect, the ſubſtance of his reflections,
upon theſe and ſome other Heads is added
in this and the following pages.

Note I.

Page 17. line 24. " There is no difficulty
" in diſcerning, that while I am ſpeaking
" in this manner, &c. "

As it has been apprehended, by a judicious friend,
that what is ſaid in this paragraph, though it is
allowed to be a ſufficient anſwer to the objection
propoſed in it, will ſcarcely be ſeen to be ſo, by
ſome perſons, without farther explication ; it may
not be amiſs to ſtate the whole affair a little more
diſtinctly ; that the miſtake of the objection, and
the force of the reply to it, may be the more eaſily underſtood.

Q The

The objection, in ſhort, is this; that if the magiſtrate has no right to lay reſtraints upon conſcience, as ſuch, wherever a plea of conſcience intervenes, his authority is at an end: that, as he can be no judge of men's hearts, whether this plea be real, or pretended, the effect which it will have upon his juriſdiction, will be the ſame: and that the greateſt crimes, by being ſheltered under this excuſe, may be committed with impunity. The inſtances, in which this inconvenience may be ſuppoſed to ariſe from liberty of conſcience, may, I preſume, be generally reduced to one of theſe caſes. The caſe of perſons, who think themſelves bound to uſe force for the propagation of what they apprehend to be truth. — The caſe of thoſe, whoſe principles lead them to judge, what are commonly thought vices hurtful to ſociety, to be innocent, and what may be indulged without ſcruple. — Or, laſtly, the caſe of thoſe, who are ſo unhappily miſled as to incorporate things hurtful to ſociety into their religion, and account it their duty to practiſe them. Theſe caſes will, in ſome circumſtances, perhaps, run one into another; but it is proper to mention them diſtinctly: and a few words, it is hoped, will make it appear, that the principles, here eſtabliſhed, neither lead to theſe evils, nor take away the power of the magiſtrate to reſtrain them.

As to the firſt of theſe caſes; that allowing every man a right to think for himſelf in matters of religion can never authorize perſons to offer violence to others, for differing from them in religion, is ſelf evident; for to affirm that it would authorize them in this, is the ſame abſurdity as ſaying, that to aſſert a right is giving power to take away that right. That any man ſhould ever attempt to uſe compulſion in religion upon the principle of every man's having a right to think for himſelf, is, at leaſt, a moral impoſſibility, if it is not a natural one. For to allow
that

that every man has a right to judge for himfelf, in matters of confcience, is allowing, almoft in exprefs terms, that confcience is not to be forced; and that a man fhould ever lay this down as the foundation, upon which he attempts to force confcience, is inconceivable. In order to juftify himfelf in fuch a conduct, he muft go upon a directly oppofite principle; and maintain that all men have NOT a right to judge for themfelves, but that fome others have a right to judge for them. If any doubt then can remain upon this head, it muft be this; why a perfon who thinks himfelf authorized to impofe his fentiments on others, fhould not be fuffered to *act* according to HIS judgment, as well as others be fuffered to *act* according to THEIRS? But the anfwer is obvious, and arifes almoft inftantaneoufly out of the premifes here mentioned: viz. becaufe his following his judgment, in this cafe, is deftructive of all the right, which others have to follow their judgments; becaufe the liberty, which he takes, is breaking in upon that liberty, which ought to be preferved in the fame extent to all; and becaufe no imaginary right, which he may arrogate to himfelf of obliging others to be directed by his judgment, can annul the real rights of others to be guided by their own. Every attack, which he makes upon their perfon, liberty or eftate, for this purpofe, is an INJURY, which comes within the limits of the civil power; and which the magiftrate is not only allowed, but is, by virtue of his office, obliged to reftrain: for conniving at thefe acts of injuftice in fome, would be a breach of his truft in behalf of others. Indeed to imagine that becaufe men have a right to be protected in acting for themfelves in religion, while they offer no injury to their fellow fubjects, therefore they muft have a right to be protected, when they do offer injuries to them; is as idle as to fuppofe, that becaufe perfons have a right to be

Q 2   fafe

safe in paffing peaceably and inoffenfively along the
publick road, they have alfo a right to be unmolefted, when they infult, and plunder all who fall
in their way.

The fame reafoning, only a little varied in the
application of it, will entirely remove this objection
alfo in the fecond cafe. Fraud, robbery, perjury,
and other crimes of the like nature, are directly
repugnant to all the effential and acquired rights
of men. Immoralities of other kinds, are acts of
injuftice to individuals, and fubverfive of the welfare
of the publick. When inftances of them occur, therefore, the magiftrate has again a right to interpofe;
and, upon the very fame principles, to correct them:
nor can this right be controuled by any pleas of
confcience, whether real or fictitious, which may be
advanced in excufe for them. The nature and confequences of the injury are what properly comes
under his infpection; and not the inward fentiment.
The violations of the rights of fociety and the members of it, are the evils, againft which he is to guard;
and, wherever thefe are to be found, he has a proper
and direct authority to check them by fuch penalties,
as their malignity, and the circumftances attending
them, require.

To enter into a particular confideration of the
third cafe, after what has been faid, would be tedi-
ous. Every intelligent reader will carry on to it,
the obfervations, which have been already made;
and the folution of it will be the fame. Religion
muft be the refult of conviction; and every man
muft, therefore, have a right, and is under an obligation, in proportion to his abilities, to judge for
himfelf in the choice of it. But if his judgment
fhould unhappily lead him to make any thing a part
of his religion, which is injurious to others, and
contrary to the fundamental laws of fociety; he fo
far ftill falls under the animadverfion of the magiftrate.

ſtrate. But then, it muſt always be remembered, that it is not becauſe the magiſtrate has an authority to dictate to conſcience, that he is thus warranted to interpoſe; but becauſe the rights of others, whom he is equally called to defend, are infringed; and the ſafety of the civil ſociety, over which he is to watch, is ſtruck at. He acts not as the dictator to his ſubjects in ſpirituals, but as the guardian of their temporalities, and the impartial protector of their civil and religious liberties. By attending to this obvious diſtinction, the rights of conſcience and the real rights of government will both be preſerved; and the pernicious extremes of calling either in queſtion will be avoided. Religious liberty will be kept from running into licentiouſneſs; civil authority be preſerved from degenerating into tyranny; and the concluſion, which has been already drawn from the whole, may be ſafely admitted; that as no man can derive from his right to follow his own conviction in religion an authority to infringe the rights of others; ſo, while he keeps clear of this, it " muſt " always remain entire to him; nor, while princi- " ples of the moſt reaſonable liberty are allowed to " ſubſiſt in their due extent, can any attempt be " conſiſtently made to take it from him." †

† Page 17, of this Eſſay.

NOTE II.

P. 57. l. 26. " What, but to join in " placing it on a more enlarged baſis, and " procuring for thoſe who requeſt it, &c."

So much has been already ſaid, in this pamphlet, to eſtabliſh this title of good ſubjects to religious liberty, that it is preſumed, in what follows, it may be conſidered as a principle, from which the diſſenters may fairly reaſon, as often as occaſions for

having

having recourfe to it may offer themfelves. It may be proper, however, to obferve here, that the very act of Toleration, the imperfection of which has been the fubject of fome of the foregoing pages, carries in it a legal acknowledgment of the right under confideration. A writer of diftinguifhed abilities, in what has been commonly called the Bangorian controverfy, afferts indeed, as I find him quoted by Bifhop *Hoadly*, " That the legiflature knows no reli- " gious rights, but what are contained in the efta- " blifhment of the church of England." What ufe was intended to be made of this affertion in that part of the controverfy, which gave occafion for them, it is not to our prefent purpofe to enquire: and that, BEFORE the Revolution, the *Legiflature* knew of no religious rights, but fuch as this writer mentions, is very willingly admitted. It was the very grievance, of which the nonconformifts, in the reigns preceding that important event, complained; that liberty of confcience, as far as law could deprive them of it, was entirely taken from them. But, at the time when the writer referred to advanced this affertion, it had been long contradicted by the voice of law. The parliament, which paffed the act of Toleration, plainly fuppofed thefe rights as the foundation, upon which they refted the fitnefs of that law; and herein all the fincere approvers of it muft concur with them. For as the excellent author, from whom I take this account of the affertions of his celebrated antagonift, juftly argues: *
" This either was the right of the diffenters, or it " was not. If it was not, then the legiflature " granted them what they had no right to, and " acted a piece of injuftice to the eftablifhed church. " But if it was their right, —— then here is a right, " and this a religious right, reftored by the means " of the Revolution, diftinct from all thofe religious " rights,

* Bp. *Hoadly*'s common rights of fubjects. P. 243.

" rights, which are implied in the eſtabliſhment of
" the church of England. The legiſlature granted
" this as a right, and a religious right : and there-
" fore, it is a groundleſs imputation upon it to ſay,
" that the legiſlature ᴋɴows no religious rights, but
" what are contained in the eſtabliſhment of the
" church, when it is ſo evident that the legiſla-
" ture ᴋɴows the right of Toleration, upon which
" the expreſs law for it muſt be ſuppoſed to be
" founded, unleſs you will ſuppoſe them to have
" done wrong to the eſtabliſhment by it." — The
force of this reaſoning, it is preſumed, will be allowed : and it is an obvious remark, that if rights of
any kind, and religious rights in particular, are
juſtly ſuppoſed in law as the ground of it, there
muſt be a degree, in which they ſubſiſt independently
of law. And if this be granted, it will ſurely be
admitted with it, that in whatever degree, reaſon
and the ſound principles of political ſocieties ſhew
them to ſubſiſt, it is fit that law ſhould allow them
to ſubſiſt alſo.

But had it ſtill been faĉt, that the legiſlature knows
no religious rights but what are contained in the
eſtabliſhment of the church of England ; what would
it have proved ? Nothing but the palpable injuſtice
of thoſe laws, which refuſed to admit ſuch rights.
During the time, in which this was really the language of the laws, the diſſenters juſtly thought
themſelves kept in a ſtate of heavy bondage
and oppreſſion ; and herein the wiſer and better
part of the nation concurred with them. There
were, even then, great numbers, who ſaw (though
ſtill, it muſt be owned, but imperfeĉtly) that there
were religious rights inherent in men, of which no
human power could juſtly attempt to deprive them.
From a ſenſe of this they more than once nobly
ſtruggled to reſcue their brethren from the ſlavery
which was entailed upon them ; and had at length
the

the pleafure to fee this deliverance take place. But had the diffenters never obtained fuch a recognition of their religious rights; would their rights have been lefs real? Or the effects of thofe, who laboured to reftore the exercife of them, lefs laudable? " To " take our notions of religious rights from human " laws, or of what Almighty God has vefted man- " kind with, from the declarations and decifions of " his fallible creatures," * (that I may again borrow the words of that able and confiftent defender of civil and religious liberty, whom I have before quoted,) to do this, I fay, is following an erroneous rule of judg- ment. " Suppofing, as he proceeds, † the legiflature " in Spain to know no religious rights, but what are " contained in the eftablifhment of the popifh church " there: will it follow, that opprefſed and injured. " proteftants there, have no fuch rights? Suppofing " the legiflature in Scotland, before the union, knew " nothing of any religious rights, but what are " contained in the eftablifhment of the KIRK of " Scotland; or that the prefent legiflature of Great- " Britain, knows nothing of any other religious " rights, in that kingdom: does it follow, that " therefore, epifcopal men, being good fubjects, have " no religious rights there? I prefume NOT." The application is obvious.

* Common rights of fubjects. p. 243.   † p. 244.

NOTE III.

P. 64. L. 2. " Is it a confequence, " that becaufe that parliament, went only " thus far, fucceeding ones muft go no " further?"

It is eafy to fee, that, if this way of reafoning were juft againft an enlargement of legal Toleration, now, it would have been equally juft immediately

after

after the Revolution, againſt any act of Toleration at all; ſince that was more than had been, till that time, granted by law. It would, I think, be very unjuſtifiable to ſuppoſe, that the author, whoſe 'reaſoning is here conſidered, entertains any diſlike to the Toleration as it now ſtands. But it may ſurely be worthy of his conſideration, whether his manner of arguing, in this part of his letter, is not, in its juſt conſequences, unfavourable to it. The diſſenters have been often condemned for ſeparating from the eſtabliſhment on account of ceremonies, forms, matters of diſcipline, and comparatively indifferent things. This ſeems, at leaſt, to be ſomething of a conceſſion, that if their diſſent was founded on points of doctrine, it would be more defenſible; and yet now that they deſire to be exempted from an obligation to ſubſcribe to the doctrinal articles of the church, they are told, that this is an indulgence never intended for them by the act of Toleration; * that it was what their predeceſſors never deſired, † and from hence it is inſinuated, that the liberty which is aſked, is too extenſive to be allowed. But, notwithſtanding the diſtinction made between theſe two caſes, the right of differing from the national eſtabliſhment in religious doctrines, and the right of differing from it in rites and ceremonies, ſtand or fall together. If the civil magiſtrate has an authority to command his ſubjects what doctrines they ſhall make a part of their religion; he has the ſame right to command what rites, and modes of worſhip they ſhall admit into it alſo. If he has no authority to oblige them to receive thoſe modes of worſhip, which he eſpouſes, he can have no authority, to oblige them to receive thoſe articles of faith, which he embraces. They have the ſame liberty, and are under the ſame obligation to enquire, and adhere to the direction of their conſciences, with

R   reſpect

* Letter to the diſſenting miniſters, p. 6.   † Ibid. p. 8.

respect to one as well as the other; and their dissenting from his judgment, in either case, can never be justly considered as an offence against his real authority; nor, while they discharge the duties of good subjects, can it be any warrant for shutting them out of his protection.

Note IV.

P. 65. l. 18. " It is no justification of " this oppression, to dignify the principles " thus enforced by penalties, with the " founding titles of doctrines, which have " been acknowledged by the christian church " in general, and the supposed fundamen- " tals of christianity."

How far this gentleman extends his notion of the unfitness of a Toleration of dissent, in points of doctrine, from the establishment, it might be running a risk of misapprehending his meaning to affirm. There is something so general, and indeterminate in his expressions, whenever he touches upon this subject, that it is difficult to see, precisely, what his idea is of it. If he thinks, however, that merely departing from established articles, is, in any case, a reason for with-holding a Toleration; he will have no reason, surely, to complain of being injured by a supposition, that he is of this opinion, in the case of a departure from, what he calls, fundamentals. * But to make a mere difference from the religion established by the magistrate, even in fundamentals, a reason for the refusal of a Toleration, is still treating Toleration, not as the right of the good citizen, but a priviledge of which he may be deprived for no offence against the community

community

* Letter, p. 8, 9.

munity, to which he belongs, but merely on account of nonconformity to the ecclefiaftical eftablifhment of it: and thus we are infenfibly brought back to the miftaken apprehenfion of a right in the magiftrate to oblige his fubjects to regulate their religious profeffion by his own. For, if, he has no authority to require their fubmiffion, to his fentiments in religion in general, he can have none to require it in fundamentals; and, if he has no right to demand it, to fay he has a right to inflict punifhment for the refufal of it, is an abfurdity. And though limiting this power in the magiftrate to the cafe of fundamentals, may feem, in a great meafure, to reftrain the exercife of it; yet, when the limitation is fearched to the bottom, it will appear to amount to very little, if to any thing at all. For, as it is left to the magiftrate to determine what are fundamentals, it will always be in his power to adjuft and enlarge the lift of them, as he judges it neceffary. Conformity to the whole fyftem of his religious opinions may be made the conditions, upon which the peace and fafety of his fubjects are to depend; and want of light, and bigotry, may lead him into all the exceffes of perfecution, which can arife from the moft arbitrary and defpotick exercife of power. It is, in reality, little more than a limitation in name; which, in effect, afferts the very thing in more plaufible language, which it is not thought expedient to maintain in plainer terms; and will, by degrees, take away all liberty of diffenting from the eftablifhed church.

But, indeed, the more I reflect on this fubject, the more I am inclinable to think, that the gentlemen, who argue in this manner, infenfibly confound fundamentals in the church, with effentials, or fundamentals in the ftate, (if the expreffion will be allowed,) and imagine that what is to be comprehended under this title in the one, muft, of courfe,

be

be fo in the other. Did not fomething of this
kind mingle itfelf with their reafonings, it feems
difficult to conceive, that perfons of fuch unqueftionable good fenfe, fhould adjuft the limits of
Toleration by a ftandard 'fo foreign to the real
principles of it. And I have the pleafure of
finding this conjecture confirmed by a very able
writer, by whofe favourable mention of this pamphlet, the author of it thinks himfelf greatly honoured, and fome of whofe words, upon this occafion, the reader will not be difpleafed to fee. The
writer, to whom I refer, is the prefent Dean of
Gloucefter, who obferves, in his letters to Dr. Kippis, * (which fell into my hands while this note
was in writing,) that it was " a pernicious maxim,
" univerfally embraced by every proteftant ftate, at
" firft, that all the members of the fame ftate
" ought, *on that very account*, to become members
" of the fame church."——" They confidered non-
" conformity to the external mode of publick wor-
" fhip, and non conformity to the civil laws of a
" country, as one and the fame thing; and, there-
" fore, they punifhed both actions on the fame
" principle. " The gentlemen, who are here concerned, do not profefs to carry this matter fo far.
They are for tolerating a diffent, but not in fundamentals. But why not in thefe, as well as in non-
fundamentals, excepting it be that, what is fundamental in the religious eftablifhment of a nation,
is fo likewife to the political fafety of it; and that
whoever departs from the one, becomes an adver-
fary to the other ? But, if this be their meaning,
it is taking that for granted, which has never yet
been proved ; nay, which may be eafily difproved.
Since nothing is eafier to conceive than, that perfons who differ from the articles of the national
church

* Page 61, 62.

church, in feveral points, thought fundamental by that church, may be, neverthelefs, unfeignedly zealous for piety, juftice, and all thofe practical principles in which the welfare of the ftate can be at all concerned. Nor is there any thing more certain, in fact, than that numbers, who have thus differed from the eftablifhed fyftem of opinions, have been eminent for their fidelity to the government, love of their country, and all thofe moral and political virtues, which are the props of civil fociety. Upon the whole, not acquiefcing even in articles, which may be deemed fundamental in religion by the formers of an ecclefiaftical eftablifhment, may be confiftent with all the duty which can be expected from the beft of fubjects; and therefore can never be a juft reafon for cutting perfons off from the religious rights of good fubjects. Where no civil duty is violated, no penalty, on a civil account, can juftly take place. It can be inflicted only on an account ftrictly ecclefiaftical, and, therefore, muft be, ftrictly and properly, perfecution.

Note V.

P. 77. After the conclufion of the note, at the bottom of this page, add as follows.

A writer in one of the publick papers, * to whom the author of this piece owns himfelf much indebted, for his civility, feems to queftion whether the doubt, to which the foregoing note relates, is a real one; and afks, whether, if it be, the author fhould not have taken this opportunity to have argued in favour of a more extenfive Toleration than the claufe in the act, referred to in the paffage to which the note is annexed, would allow, provided it fhould

not

* London Chronicle, Dec. 22—24, 1772.

not be affected by the words of the bill prefented
by the diffenters? In anfwer to the firft of thefe
particulars, the author affures him, that the doubt
was a real one. In anfwer to the fecond, the writer
of the letter is defired to confider, that the bufinefs
of this treatife, in this part of it, was only to enquire, whether the confequence charged upon the
bill in queftion, would, in fact, have followed from
it, if it had paffed; and to fhew that if the confequence really followed from it, with refpect to the
act of Toleration, there were other equivalent, and
more than equivalent legal fecurities of the honour
of the eftablifhed doctrine and worfhip of the church
of England, which would not have been affected
by the liberty requefted by the diffenters; and as
this was the author's only view, in this place, this
was all which he thought it neceffary to fay here
upon the fubject. But endeavouring to fhew that an
objection is made without foundation in fact, is,
by no means admitting that, if it had been otherwife, it would have been of fufficient force to anfwer the end for which it is produced. It is rea-
dily agreed, with the writer, for the removal of
whofe doubts this paragraph is inferted; that the
followers of Athanafius, Arius, Arminius, and Soci-
nus, may, all of them, be equally good fubjects;
and, as fuch, equally entitled to the protection of
the magiftrate in their refpective religious perfua-
fions. No judicious friend of truth will object to
having any human expofitions of the articles of
revelation, left open to fober and candid difcuffion;
nor do the gentlemen, who are defirous to have
fuch enquiries reftrained by worldly terrors, if any
fuch there be, at all confult the honour and fafety
of the doctrines, for which they are fo tenderly
concerned. "If there be a way upon earth," as it
has juftly been obferved, "to render a doctrine fuf-
"pected, it is to enforce the belief of it by pains

"and

" and penalties." If the doctrines of a national
religion are founded in truth, they will stand; and
neither argument, nor ridicule, (how improper so-
ever the use of it on such subjects may be) will
be able to subvert them. If they are not founded in truth, their sincerest defenders will not wish
them to stand; nor will it be in the power of penal laws always to support them.—The author
speaks not this in the character of an enemy to
the doctrines of the articles, with the merits of
which his book does not require him to intermed-
dle. His concern in it is not with the truth and
falshood of opinions, but with the principles and
just extent of religious liberty; and he thinks it
an happiness, that, for the justification of his zeal
in favour of so excellent a cause, he need look no
farther than the authority of a late very celebrated writer, whose words, in his letter to Horace
Walpole, Esq; concerning American Bishops, p. 23,
it may not be improper to repeat. " It is not
" merely from my attachment to the church of En-
" gland, that I am a favourer of the scheme in
" question: but from my love of RELIGIOUS LIBER-
" TY; which, in this point, the members of the
" church of England, in our colonies, do not en-
" joy." Whether, from the same principles, the
dissenters are not justified in their application, the
reader is left to judge.

NOTE VI.

P. 87. l. 9. " He owns, indeed, the
" MERIT of several among them, with a
" politeness, which entitles him to their
" most respectful acknowledgments; &c."

Great stress is laid by the author of the letter
to the dissenting ministers upon the opposition, which
the

the diffenters are fuppofed to have made to the fcheme of eftablifhing bifhops in America; and he fpeaks as if it had been confidered as almoft decifive againft them. The impreffion which this reprefentation of the conduct of the diffenters might make is not here difputed. — The juftice of the charge againft the diffenters, it is ftill expected, will be examined by a better pen. But if it is this writer's defign to infinuate that the diffenters, and efpecially their minifters in general, are concerned to hinder their epifcopal brethren abroad, from enjoying the advantages of the defired inftitution, he is much a ftranger to their difpofition. Dr. Furneaux's letters which were appealed to as a witnefs in this cafe againft the diffenters, contain a fufficient teftimony for them, * that with proper fecurity for the liberty of thofe of other denominations, they will be fo far from oppofing, that they will be advocates for fuch a fcheme. But were the fact otherwife; the ufe made of it by this writer, in the affair under confideration, is, in the judgment of the lately quoted primate of the church, a very unjuftifiable one. He fays, indeed, † " that he cannot imagine how the " diffenters can pretend to be lovers of [religious " liberty,] and wifh it to be with-held from their " fellow fubjects." But admit they fhould; what is his reflection ? " God forbid that we fhould ever " be moved by THIS, OR ANY OTHER PROVOCA- " TION, to wifh it with-held IN ANY INSTANCE " WHATEVER from the diffenters ! " ‡

* P. 191. 2d edit.   † Letters to Horace Walpole. p. 23.
‡ Ibid. p. 24.

THE END.

www.ingramcontent.com/pod-product-compliance
Lightning Source LLC
Chambersburg PA
CBHW021120020726
47500CB00003B/848